(कृण्वन्तो विश्वमार्यम्—ऋ. 9.63.5)
(*Let the whole world be civilised - RV. 9.63.5*)

India
The Cradle of World Civilizations

By

Dr. Ravi Prakash Arya

INDIAN FOUNDATION FOR VEDIC SCIENCE
H.O.1051, Sector-1, Rohtak, Haryana, India Ph. 01262-292580
Delhi Contact Ph. Nos.: 09313033917; 09650183260
Emails: vedicscience@rediffmail.com; vedicscience@hotmail.com
Website : www.vedascience.com

First Edition

Kali era: 5015 (c. 2014)
Kalpa era: 1,97,29,49,115
Brahma era: 15,50,21,97,9,49,115

ISBN No. 81-87710-68-3

© Author

Contents

Preface

This book digs deep into the past of the world. It is a collection of the findings of various scholars who tried to search the ancient world without any prejudice and preconceived notions or racial or colonial biases. Presently, due to the false propaganda by the pseudo historians, the genuine and impartial authors have been marginalised and so have gone into oblivion. Such great authors are neither highlighted nor referred to by the coming generations of authors. This book is intended to bring into limelight the contribution of true researchers and discoverers of the past of the world. It is a matter of great concern and disappointment that today in the name of writing history of the past in a systematic and scientific manner, the traces of the history of the past are being obliterated in a very systematic and scientific manner. Satanic forces have always tried to darken the history of civilisation. Who can forget those dark events of the human history and civilisation when Alexandrian library, libraries of Nalanda, Vikramshila Ujjain were set to fire.

It is all the more disgusting to know that today also when the humanity has risen from the slumber of ignorance, the same type of forces are at work in the different tribal areas of the world. The tribal population in Asia, Africa, Australia and South America is constantly being raided and raped with ulterior motives. If they are gaining bread at one hand, they are losing their historical roots on the other hand. They are paying a high cost of their true history for the satiation of their hunger. No doubt the need of history comes after satiation of hunger, but by the time hunger will be satiated, the roots will be ruined. This is a kind of trajectory in which world's past has been constructed. Historical reality is already very difficult to map. But the mapping becomes more difficult when the motivations and moulds are racist, colonial and communal. Under the circumstances the intellectual myopia rules the roost and the squinted eye reveals in the glory, might and prosperity of one's own self to the utter neglect of the 'other'. The 'other' then appears barbarian, vulgar, dwarfed and depraved, and the squinted eye is, at best, able to wink mainly on the muck and morass associated with the 'other'.

The present book is a humble attempt to fight the above situation. Indian Foundation for Vedic Science in association with like-minded organisations like International Vedic Vision in New York and International Foundation for Vedic Science in Canada has taken a lead in the direction of reconstruction of the obliterated past of the world. The canvas of the world history needs to be enlarged with a vast corpus of historical literature that has been churned out from time to time by a wide variety of scholars, historians, researchers and research institutes, and not with the help of excavated debris, fossils and skeletons. History is neither a story book to be fabricated on the heap of garbage nor a work of jigsaw fit done from the collection of some relics retained at Kabari's shop. History deals with the past of living human-beings and should preferably be written on the basis of records either written in the literary form or carried forward from generations to generations in the oral tradition of ballads, folk lores and folk songs. The countries who do not have any historical literature or oral historical tradition, can construct their past with help of their reminisces retained in the historical records of other countries.

Dr. Ravi Prakash Arya
114-Akash, DRDO Complex,
Lucknow Road, Timarpur, Delhi-110054 (India)
Ph. +91 9313033917

I
Introduction
(India - The Civiliser of the World)

Louis Jacolliot in the preface to his book 'La Bible Dans L'Inde' observes as follows :

India is the world's cradle; thence it is, that the common mother in sending forth her children even to the utmost West, has in unfading testimony of our origin bequeathed us the legacy of her language, her laws, her morale, her literature, and her religion.

Traversing Persia, Arabia, Egypt, and even forcing their way to the cold and cloudy North, far from the sunny soil of their birth; in vain they may forget their point of departure, their skin may remain brown, or become white from contact with snows of the West; of the civilisations founded by them splendid kingdoms may fall, and leave no trace behind but some few ruins of sculptured columns; new peoples may rise from the ashes of the first; new cities flourish on the site of the old; but time and ruin united fail to obliterate the even legible stamp of origin.

"Science now admits, as a truth needing no further demonstration, that all the idioms of antiquity were derived from the far East; and thanks to the labours of Indian philologists, our modern languages have found their derivation and their roots in Sanskrit."

"It was but yesterday that the lamented Burnouf drew the attention of his class to our much better comprehension of the Greek and Latin, since we have commenced the study of Sanskrit."

"And do we not now assign the same origin to Slavonic and Germanic languages?" She further observes,

"Manu inspired Egyptian, Hebrew, Greek, and Roman legislation, and his spirit still permeates the whole economy of our European laws."

Jacolliot quotes Cousin who said, **"The history of Indian philosophy is the abridged history of the philosophy of the world."**

But this is not all. In the words of Jacolliot:

The emigrant Indians, together with their laws, their usage, their customs, and their language, carried with them equally their religion – their pious memories of the Gods of that home which they were to see no more – of those domestic gods whom they had burnt before leaving forever.

So in returning to the fountain-head, do we find in India all the poetic and religious traditions of ancient and modern peoples? The worship of Zoroaster, the symbols of Egypt, the mysteries of Eleusis and the priestesses of Vesta, the Genesis and prophecies of the Bible, the morale of the Samian sage, and the sublime teachings of the philosopher of Bethlehem.

This book comes to familiarise all those truths which have hitherto but agitated the higher regions of thought, those truths which, doubtless, many have perceived without daring to proclaim them.

It tries to trace the history of origin and development of civilisations in the world. This is not the first attempt. Many scholars from time to time have been unravelling mysteries of the past traversing the same path. The present author make an humble attempt to pool the whole data that is likely to sink into oblivion and fizzle out from the gaze of all and present the same before readers afresh in the ensuing pages. The findings presented in this book are sure to reverse the trend of modern history and compel the genuine readers, researchers and scholars to rediscover and reconstruct the past of the world. The collection of views in the present book lays the foundation of Indo-centric world view and sets aside the Euro-centric view of looking at the past of the world. When the readers will gaze the past of world through eyes of Vedas and Vedic scholars like Swami Dayananda Saraswati and other scholars like Louis Jacolliot, Pococke, William Jones, Tod, Count Bjornstjerna, Elphinston, Eurebius, Heeren, Coleman, Pt. Bhagvadatta, Yudhisthira Mimansaka, Pt. Guruddata, Gurudatta Vidyarthi, Harbilas Sarda and P.N. Oak, they are certainly not going to have any choice but to join the above mentioned scholars in holding India the centre of learning and civilisation and paying tribute to her (India's) contribution for development modern civilisation and humanity in the gracious utterances of the seeker of truth (Louis Jacolliot) :

> **Soil of Ancient India, cradle of humanity, hail! Hail, venerable and efficient nurse whom centuries of brutal invasions have not yet buried under the dust of oblivion, hail, father land of faith, of love, of poetry and of science. May we hail a revival of thy past in our Western future!**

The venerable author was quite conscious of the results of her acknowledgement to the contribution of India to the world civilisation and humanity in the 19th century. The present author cannot avoid quoting her fear of consequences of the publication/ proclamation of her true findings with regard to world history in general and history of Europe and India in particular. She expresses her fear as follows:

> **Aware of the resentment I am provoking, I yet shrink not from the encounter. We are no longer burnt at the stake, as in the times of Michael Servetus, Savonarola, and of Philip II. of Spain; and**

**free thought may be freely proclaimed in an
atmosphere of freedom. And thus do I submit my
book to the reader.**

The above fear expressed by the author, not only
reflect the true picture of the process of distorting but
also dewriting the actual history of the world by
tempering with the data and negating the Indian tradition
of origin and history of humankind on the globe in the
name of emerging science and technology.

This introduction will not be complete until and
unless the reminisces of Louis Jacolliot during his stay in
India are not shared with the readers. He says :

I have dwelt midst the depths of your mysterious
forests, seeking to comprehend the language of your
lofty nature, and the evening airs that murmured midst
the foliage of banyans words : Zeus, Jehova, Brahma.

I have inquired of priests under the porches of temples
and ancient pagodas; and they have replied, "To live is
to think, to think is to study God, who is all, and is in
all."

I have listened to the instruction of scholars and sages,
and they have said, "To live is to learn, to learn is to
examine and to fathom in all their perceptible forms the
innumerable manifestation of celestial power."

I have turned to philosophers and have said to them :
What then are you doing here, stationary, for more than
six thousand years, and what is this book that you are
always fumbling on your knees? And they have smiled
in murmuring these words, "To live is to be useful, to
live is to be just, and we learn to be useful and just in
studying this book of the Vedas, which is the word of
eternal wisdom, the principle of principles as revealed
to our fore-fathers."

I have heard the songs of poets – and love, beauty,

perfumes and flowers, they too have afforded their divine instruction.

I have seen fakirs smiling at grief on a bed of thorns and of burning coals – suffering spoke to them of God.

I have ascended to the sources of the Ganges, where thousands of Hindus kneel, at the sun's rising, on the banks of the sacred river and the breeze has borne to me these words, "The fields are green with rice, and the coca- tree bends under its fruit – let us return thank to Him who gave them."

And yet this earnest faith, these breathing beliefs, despite the sublime instruction of Indian scholars, of sages, of philosophers and of poets, I have seen your sons, poor old Hindu mother, enervated, enfeebled, demoralised by brutish passions, abandon, without complaint to a handful of grinding merchants, your blood, your wealth, your virgin daughters, and your liberty.

How often have I not hear on the evening air, hoarse moans of wailing complaint that seemed to rise from desert marshes, sombre pathways, rivers' banks, or woody shades, etc. Was it the voice of the past, returning to weep o'er a lost civilisation and an extinguished grandeur?

Was it the expiring groan of Sepoys mowed down pell-mell by grape with their wives and children after the revolt, by some red-jackets who thus revenged their own panic?

Was it the wail of nurselings, vainly seeking sustenance at the cold breast of mothers - dead from starvation?

Alas! what fearful sufferings has it been my fate to witness!

A people smiling in apathy under the iron hand that destroys them, and with their own hand joyously digging the grave of their ancient glories, of their recollections and of their independence.

What sinister influence, I asked myself, has then been the cause of such a state of decomposition? Is it simply the work of time, and is it the destiny of nations, as of man, to die of decrepitude?

How is it that the primeval doctrines, the sublime instruction of the Vedas have ended in such a failure?

And still I heard scholars and sages, philosophers and poets - *in solemn converse* - on the immortality of the soul, on the great social virtues, and on the Divinity!

And still I saw the populations bend before Him who gave them cloudless sun and fertile soil!

At least, however, I perceived that it was, alas! but an empty form. .. And I saw with sadness that these people had bartered the spirit of their sublime beliefs for a verbal fanaticism, freedom of thought and the free will of free men for the blind and stolid submission of the slave.

Then it was that I sought to lift the obscuring veil from the past, and backwards trace the origin of this dying people, who without energy for either hatred or affection, without enthusiasm for either virtue or vice, seem to personate an actor doomed to act out his part before an audience of Statues.

How glorious the epoch that then presented itself to my study and comprehension! I made tradition speak from the temple's recess, I inquired of monuments and ruins, I questioned the Vedas whose pages count their existence by thousands of years, and whence inquiring youth imbibed the science of life long before Thebes of the hundred gates or Babylon the great had traced out their foundations.

I listened to recitals of those ancient poems which were

sung at the feet of Brahmā when the shepherds of Upper Egypt and of Judea had not yet been born. . . . I sought to understand those laws of Manu which were administered by Indians under the porches of pagodas ages and ages before the tables of the Hebrew law had descended midst thunders and lightning from the heights of Sinai.

And then did India appear to me in all the living power of her originality – I traced her progress in the expansion of her enlightenment over the world - I saw her giving her laws, her customs, her morale and her religion to Egypt, to Persia, to Greece and to Rome – I saw Jaiminī and Veda-Vyāsa precede Socrates and Plato, - and Christana (Krishna), the son of Devakī, precede the son of the Virgin of Bethlehem.

This was the epoch of greatness, under the regime of reason.

And then I followed the footsteps of decay . . . old age approached there people who had instructed the world, and impressed upon it their morale and their doctrines with a seal so ineffaceable, that time, which has entombed Babylon and Nineveh, Athens and Rome, has not yet been able to obliterate it.

I saw Brahmins and priests lend the sacerdotal support of voice and sacred function to the stolid despotism of kings – and ignoring their own origin, stifle India under a corrupt theocracy that soon extinguished the liberty that would have been its overthrow, as the memory of those past glories which were its reproach.

And then I saw clearly why there people, after two thousand years of religious thraldom, were powerless to repulse their destroyers and demand retribution, bowing passively to the hated domination of English merchants –while night and morning on bent knees imploring that God in whose name Sacerdotalism had effected their ruin.

Tunnel view of the Founders of Euro-centric view of World History

Louis Jacolliot is among the first few scholars who conceded the truth that India was cradle of civilisation. She proclaims as follows : **"India - by her language, her usage, her laws, and her historic traditions, the civiliser of the world."**

She is able to visualise that the European scholarship suffering from superiority complex could not tolerate Indian superiority and tried to conceal and overlook the facts in the light of their tunnel vision. She highlights this tunnel vision of Europeans and founders of Euro-centric view of world history. He observes at length:

> The Europeans when first set foot upon the soil of India, proud of the history and civilisation of their father-land and crammed with extravagant prejudices, come fully persuaded that bring with him a morality the most lofty, a philosophy the most rational, and a religion the most pure: and then witnessing the impotent toils of Christian missionaries, who with difficulty assemble their few pariah proselytes, murmurs his scorn of semi-brutalised fanaticism and returns to his country, after having witnessed some ceremonies which he did not understand, seen some monstrous idols that made him shrug his shoulders, and some Fakirs, a species of Simon Stylites, whose self-tortures and flagellation filled him with disgust.

> If an unhappy devotee with difficulty raised himself from the steps of a temple dedicated to Viṣṇu or to Śiva to solicit alms, he has perhaps looked at him with pity while murmuring the articles of our code against vagabondage, and yet in visiting Rome he may possibly have dropped some few oboli into the trembling hand of the more fortune *Joseph Labre*, the Fakir of the West.

Very few travellers have sought to understand India, very few have submitted to the labour necessary to a knowledge of her past splendours, looking only at the surface they have even denied them, and with an unreasoning confidence of criticism that made them the easy victims of ignorance.

What is the use of Sanskrit?", cries Jocquemont, and proud of his own flippancy proceeds to construct a conventional East which his successors have copies, which all libraries have adopted, and which is even to-day the source of all the errors that constitute three-fourths of the amount of Europe's knowledge of that country.

And yet, what hidden wealth to be unveiled! What treasures of literature, of history, of morale and philosophy to be made known to the world!

The labours of Strange, of Colebrooke, of William Jones, of Weber, Lassen, and Burnouf, have thrown some light upon all these things. **Let us hope that a succession of Orientalist may follow, and succeed in completely reconstructing an epoch which would find nothing to envy in the grandeur and civilisation of our own, and which initiated the world in all the great principles of legislature, of morale, of philosophy, and of religion**.

Louis Jacolliot feels that Sanskrit is only the channel of communication with the past of the world. A historian devoid of the knowledge of Sanskrit is blind and the Oriental scholar (Sanskrit scholar) in the west who has not lived in India is lame. Such a historian and Sanskrit scholar can never do justice with the past of the world. Mindful of this hard fact Jacolliot observes as follows :

Unhappy it is almost impossible to retrace the infancy of this mysterious country without domestication in it, without familiarity with its manners, its customs, and above all without deep knowledge of Sanskrit, the language of its youth, and of Tamil, its living learned language, our only channel of communication with the past.

My complaint against many translators and Orientalists, while admiring their profound knowledge is, that not having lived in India, they fail in exactness of expression and in comprehension of the symbolic sense of poetic chants, prayers, and ceremonies, and thus too often fall into material errors, whether of translation or appreciation.

I have scarce found any but the productions of the illustrious Englishmen, William Jones and Colebrook, admitted by Indian scholars to be exact interpretations of their works, a fact which they attributed to the residence of these learned men amongst then; seeking their assistance and profiting by their instruction. Few writers are, in fact, so cloudy and obscure as the Indians; their thought must be disengaged from an atmosphere of poetic ornament, rhetorical flourish, and religious invocation, which certainly do not tend to elucidate the subject treated. **Again, the Sanskrit, for every variety of image or idea, has number-less different forms of expression which have no equivalent in our modern languages, which can only be rendered by great circumlocution, requiring that intimate knowledge only to be acquired from the soil, the manner, customs, laws, and religious traditions of the people whose origin we study and whose works we translate.**

To fathom ancient India, all knowledge acquired in Europe avails naught; the study must re-commence, as the child learns to read, and the harvest is too distant for lukewarm energies.

But, then, how brilliant the spectacle at last presented to our view, and how ample the reward of perseverance!

Writers, Savants interested in India, come and live with the Indian in his huts; come and learn his ancient language, assist at his ceremonies, his chants, his prayers; theologians, study Brahma and his worship, Vedic scholars will instruct you in the Vedas and the laws of Manu; revel midst remains of a literature the most ancient, examine still-existing structures, the legacies of earliest ages, and which stand in their symbolic architecture as monuments of an extinguished grandeur midst decay that nothing can arrest, for it is the law of destiny - of inexorable fate.

Then you will have been initiated, and India will appear to you the mother of human race - the cradle of all or traditions.

The life of several generations would scarce suffice merely to read the works that ancient India has left us on history, morale, poetry, philosophy, religion, different sciences, and medicine; gradually each will produce its contribution, – for sciences too possesses faith to move mountains, and renders those whom it inspires capable of the greatest sacrifices.

A society in Bengal has assumed the mission of collecting and translating the Vedas.

We shall discover whence Moses and the Prophets abstracted their Holy Scripture, and perhaps restore their book of Kings, which they report lost, but which I am of opinion they never possessed, and could not transcribe for their Bible from mere tradition.

It may be said that I make my debut with strange propositions. Patience; multiplied proofs will present themselves, redoubling and sustaining each other.

And perhaps it is here that the ruling idea of this work should be declared. It is this.

In this same manner as modern society jostles antiquity at each step – as our poets have copied Homer and

Virgil, Sophocles and Euripides, Plautus and Terence; as our philosophers have drawn inspiration from Socrates, Pythagoras, Plato and Aristotle; as our historians take Titus Livius, Sallust, or Tacitus as models; our orators Demosthenes or Cicero; our physicians study Hippocrates, and our codes transcribe Justinian – so had antiquity's self also an antiquity to study, to imitate, and to copy. What more simple and more logical?... Do not peoples precede and succeed each other? Does the knowledge painfully acquired by one nation confine itself to its own territory, and die with the generation that produced it? **Can there be any absurdity in the suggestion that the India of six thousand years ago, brilliant, civilised, overflowing with population, impressed upon Egypt, Persia, Judea, Greece, and Rome a stamp as ineffaceable, impressions as profound, as these last have impressed upon us?**

It is time to disable ourselves of those prejudices which represent the ancients as having almost spontaneously elaborated ideas, philosophic, religious, and moral, the most lofty – these prejudices that in their native admiration explain all in the domain of science arts, and letters by the intuition of some few great men, and in the realm of religion by revelation.

And because we have for ages lost the connecting links between antiquity, so called, and India, is that a sufficient reason for still worshipping a delusion without seeking its possible solution?

Have we not, in disruption with the past, by experiment, by the scales and crucible, refuted occult mediaeval sciences?

Let us then carry the same principle of experiment into the realm of thought. Philosophers, let us reject intuition! Rationalists, let us repudiate revelation!

I ask of all who have specially studied antiquity if it has

not twenty times occurred to them that these people must have drunk form some spring Pierian unknown to us? When posed by some point of historic or philosophic obscurity, if they have not twenty times said to themselves, "Ah ! if the Alexandrian Library had not been burnt, perhaps we might there have found the lost secret of the past."

One thing always especially struck me. We know by what studies our thinkers, our moralists, our legislators, have formed themselves. But who were the precursors of Menes the Egyptian, of Moses, of Socrates, of Plato, and of Aristotle?

Who, lastly, was the precursor of Christ?

Will it be said they had no precursors?

I reply that my reason rejects the spontaneity of intelligence, -- the intuition of these men, which some explain as divine revelation!

And escaping from the cloudy past, I accept freely reasoned criticism alone in my forward progress on that road which, to my thought at least, must lead at last to the goal of truth.

Nations only attain éclat after long and painful infancy, unless aided by the light of peoples that have preceded them.

Remember how modern society groped in darkness until the fall of Constantinople restored the light of antiquity.

The Indian emigration rendered the same service to Egypt, to Persia, Judea, Greece, and Rome, is what I propose to demonstrate.

Certainly I do not promise as complete elucidation as I could wish; the task is beyond the power of a single worker. I present an idea which I believe true-supported by such proofs as I have been able to collect as well from the works of learned Orientals, as from my own feeble resources – others will explore the mine, better, perhaps, and more deeply – in the meantime, behold the first *coup de pioche.*

And I must here, once for all, declare that I seek neither contest nor offence; that possessing the most prefect respect for all beliefs, I yet hold myself free absolutely to reject them in my entire independence of thought.

Enquirers who have adopted Egypt as their field of research, and who have explored and re-explored that country from temple to tomb, would have us believe it the birthplace of our civilisation. There are some who even pretend that India adopted from Egypt her casts, her language, and her laws, while Egypt is on the contrary but one entire Indian emanation.

They have every advantage, the encouragement of Government, the support of learned societies; but, patience! the light will appear. If India is too far off for lukewarm energies, if its sun kills, and its Sanskrit is too difficult for a little possible charlatanism, if it has no fund for transporting defaced blocks of stone; there are, on the other side, some few believers for whom India is a religion, who work without ceasing, not at excavating ditches and turning up sand, but at exhuming, studying, and restoring books. Ere long they will establish the proposition as a truism – that to study India is to trace humanity to its sources.

No Greek Invasion in India

Louis Jacolliot doesn't find any Greek invasion or Alexander's presence in India. He observes :

Other writers dazzled with admiration of Hellenic light find it everywhere, and give themselves up to absurd theories.

M. Philarete Chasles, in his book on the East, assumed as a result of Alexander's almost legendary inroad into Northern India, that Greek influence had diffused throughout the whole country and vivified ancient Indian civilisation, arts, and literature, which is about as logical as to maintain that the Saracen invasion of the time of Charles Martel had some influence on the Gauls anterior to the Roman Conquest.

Such an opinion is a simple chronological absurdity.

At the epoch of Alexander, India has already passed the period of her splendour, and was sinking into decay; her great achievements in philosophy, morals, literature, and legislation already counting more than two thousand years of existence; and further, I defy whoever he may be, to show in India the faintest trace, the most insignificant vestige, whether in their different idioms, their usage, their literature, their ceremonies, or their religion, to indicate the presence of the Greek.

Jacolliot says, "The presence of Alexander in India was but a brutal fact isolated circumscribed, exaggerated by Hellenic tradition, which the Indians have not even deigned to record in their history. I would not unwillingly wound a writer whose talents I sincerely admire, but I cannot forbear telling him that it is a dream hatched at the hazard of the pen, a paradox incapable of sustaining even a semblance of discussion, and to which I am truly astonished that a distinguished Orientalist, M. du Menil, I believe, should have given himself the trouble seriously to reply."

"To pretend today – in the absence of all proof, and while we find not in the annals of India even the Hellenicised name of the conquered Porus – that Athens inspired Indian genius, as she gave life to European art, is to ignore the history of India – to make the parent the pupil of the child; in fact, it is to forget Sanskrit."

Sanskrit as the Proof of Indian Origin of races of Europe, and of India's Maternity

The Sanskrit is itself the most irrefutable and most simple proof of the Indian origin of the races of Europe, and of India's maternity."

Jacolliot accepts this fact and says :

To individuals, what I am about to say may be nothing new; but let them not forget that in propounding a perhaps new idea, I avail myself of all discoveries that seem to support it, with the view of familiarising, and making known to the masses who have neither means nor time for such studies, that extra ordinary pristine civilisation which we have never yet surpassed.

If the Sanskrit formed the Greek, as in fact all other languages ancient and modern (of which I shall presently offer many proofs), it could only have been conveyed to these different countries by successive emigrations; it would be absurd to suppose otherwise; and history, although groping its way on this subject, rather aids than opposes this hypothesis.

This granted, with so finished a language, we must conclude that the people who spoke it had attained a high degree of civilisation, and that with their mother-tongue they also necessarily preserved their historic and religious traditions, literature, and legislation.

If the language, in spite of its many mutations, and after

Ariadne – The unhappy princess abandoned by Theseus, and who had committed the fault of giving herself up to enemy of her family; In Sanskrit, *Ari-ana-* seduced by an enemy.

Rhadamanthus – Another Judge in Hell, in mythology; in Sanskrit, *Radha-manta* – who chastises crime.

Andromeda – Scarified to Neptune, and succored by Presence. In Sanskrit, *Andh-ra-medha* – scarified to the passion of the Water God.

Persius – In Sanskrit, *Para-saha* – timely succour.

Oresters – Celebrated for his madness. In Sanskrit, *O-raksa-ta* – devoted to misfortune.

Pylades – Then friend of Orestes. In Sanskrit, *Pula-da* – who connsoles by his friendship.

Aphigenia – The sacrificed virgin. In Sanskrit, Apha-gana- who ends without posterity.

Centaur – Mythologic, half man, half horse. In Sanskrit, Ken-tura. Man-horse.

The Olympian divinities have the same origin:

Jupiter – In Sanskrit, *Zu-pitr*, Father of Heaven, or *Zeus-pitri*, of which the Greeks have made the word Zeus, and he Hebrews Jehovah.

Pallas – The Goddess of Wisdom. In Sanskrit, *Pala-sa* – protecting wisdom.

Athenia – The Greek Goddess of Chastity. In Sanskrit, *A-tanaya* – without children.

Minerva – Who is the same goddess with the Romans but with added attribute of courage. In Sanskrit, *Ma-nara-va* – who supports the strong.

Bellona – Goddess of war. In Sanskrit, Bala-na – warlike

strength.

Neptune – In Sanskrit, Na-pata-na- who governs the furious waves.

Poseidon – Another Greek name of Neptune. In Sanskrit, *Pasa-uda* - who calms the waters.

Mars – God of War. In Sanskrit, *Mri-* who gives death.

Pluto – God of Hell. In Sanskrit, *Plushta* - who strikes with fire.

A few examples now from among the people; there is no better way of proving emigration than by the etymology of names.

The Pelasgi – In Sanskrit, *Palāśa-ga-* who fight without pity.

The Leleges – In Sanskrit, *Lala-ga-* who march spreading fear.

How well the signification of these words accord with the taste of young and warlike people for giving themselves names in harmony with their habits!

The Hellenes – In Sanskrit, *Hela-na-* worriors, worshippers of the moon. Does not Greece also call herself Hellas?

The Spartans – In Sanskrit, *Spardha-ta---* the rivals.

And these Sanskrit words which, passing into Greece, have become the names of celebrated men:

Pythagoras – In Sanskrit, *Pith-guru-* the school-master.

Anaxagoras – In Sanskrit, *Anaṅga guru* – the spirit-master.

Protagoras – *Prata-guru* – the master distinguished in all sciences.

If we pass from Greece into Italy, Gaul, Germany, and Scandinavia, we find the same Sanskrit origins :

The Italians – From Italus, son of a Trojan hero. In Sanskrit, *Itala* – men of low castes.

The Bretii – *Bharata,* people of the artisan castes.

The Tyrrhenians – *Tyra-na,* swift warriors.

The Sabines – *Sabha-na*, the warrior caste.

The Samnites – *Samna-ta*, the banished.

Te Celtes – *Kalla-ta,* the invading chiefs.

The Gauls – *Ga-lata,* people who conquer as they march.

The Belge – *Bala-ja,* children of the strong.

The Sequanes – *Saka-na,* superior warriors.

The Sicambres – *Su-kam-bri,* good lords of the land.

The Scandinavians – *Skanda-nava,* worshippers of Skanda, the God of Battles.

Odin – *Yodhin,* a warrior.

The Swede – *Su-yodha,* good soldier.

Norway – *Nara-vaja,* the country of mariners, or men of the sea.

The Baltic – *Bala-ta-ka,* sea of the powerful conquerors.

The Alamanni (Germans) – *Ala-manu,* free men.

The Valaques – In Sanskrit, *Vala-ka,* the servile class.

The Moldavians – *Mal-dha-va,* people of the lowest caste.

Ireland – *Erin,* rocks surrounded with salt water.

Thane (or ancient Scottish chief) – *Tha-na,* chief of warriors.

In Asia, the whole dynasty of the Xerxes and the Artaxerxes is of Indian origin. All the names of strong places, of cities, of countries, are nearly pure Sanskrit. Here are a few examples:

MA – The lunar Divinity of all the tribes of Asia and of the East. In Sanskrit, *Ma,* the moon.

Artaxerxes – *Artha-kṣatrias,* The Great King. Was he not so called by the Greeks?

Mesopotamia – *Madya-potama,* country between rivers.

Castabala (strong place) – *Kāṣṭha-bala,* impenetrable strength.

Zoroaster (who brought sun-worship into Asia). Sanskrit, *Sūrya-stare*, who teaches sun-worship.

This is enough; it would require volumes properly to treat this philological question; moreover, it is quite common to trace to Sanskrit all ancient and modern languages; the affiliation is so clear, so precise, as to forbid even a shadow of doubt.

Some names from fabulous and heroic times, and from the principal peoples, ancient and modern, have been quoted above.

None of these names of heroes, of gods, of warriors, philosophers, countries, or peoples, have any signification of construction in the languages to which they belong, and as it would be absurd to attribute them to chance, the most simple and most rational solution is to assign them to the Sanskrit, which not only explains them in their grammatical origin, but also in their symbolic or real sense, historic or figurative.

Thus the populations of Indian origin, Ionians, Dorians, and others, pass from Asia Minor to colonise

Greece; they bring their cradle-recollections, all the traditions that poetry had preserved to them, no doubt with modifications; but also leaving them a stamp so special, that it is possible for us to recover and to explain them to-day, through the ages, which passing over all these things have fatally enveloped them in obscurity and oblivion.

Midst the souvenirs of these colonists of a new soil, appear in the first rank the innumerable exploits of the god of war of their ancestors the Indians, that is Śiva; they forget the name of this God, who does not even possess warlike attributes in the mythology of Upper Asia, and preserve to him only the epithet Hara-Kala, which Indian poets give him when he presides over war. According to Louis Jacolliot :

> Hara-Kala, the hero of battles, becomes Hercules is also etymolised as Hara-kula-es, meaning 'chief of the tribe of Śiva' and the new community adopts him under that name, and Greek, like Indian fable, continues to make him the destroyer of lions, of serpents, of hydras, and even of entire armies; it is only the tradition that continues itself.

> Zeus, God, the name of the Indian Trinity; Brahma, Viṣ ṇu, Śiva, is preserved without alteration.

> Thc-Saha, the associate of Śiva, becomes Theseus.

> Aha-ka, Radha-Manta, Manarava, A-tanaya, Napatana, Bala-na, Palasa, Andha-ra-meda, Ari-ana, become Æacus, Rhada-manthus, Minerva, Athenaia, Neptune, Bellona, Pallas Andro-meda, and Ariadne.

> Brahmā, also called Dyaus-pitṛ, Father of heavens, becomes Jupiter; and if this word may be dissevered in Greek, preserving the sense, it is that this language has retained almost in their purity the two Sanskrit words of which it is formed- Zeus and Pitṛ, in Greek, Zeus and

Pater. Prata-guru, and Ananga-guru, become Protagoras and Anaxagoras- these names are not proper names, but qualities descriptive of men who have distinguished themselves in science and philosophy; and Pythagoras, derived from Pitha-guru, still better proclaims its Indian origin, in propagating in Greece the Indian system of metempsychosis.

And so of the rest, all the names of antique fable have the same Indian affinity of signification and of origin. It would be easy to follow the scent, to de-compound all, and assign them their etymology of words and of meaning, if that were the principal object of this work.

As indicated above, if one digs deeper in this mine. There is here an immense field for exploration by the learned.

What has been said of the names of heroes and demi-gods of ancient Greece, applies equally to the names of more modern peoples, of which also some etymologies have been given by Louis Jacolliot, such as the Bretii, the Tyrrhenians, Samnites, Celts, Gauls, Sequares, Scambres, Scandinavians, Belge, Norwegians, Germans, Wallachs, Moldavians, etc. ... In view of the above similarity of Roman and Greek names with Sanskrit, Louis Jacolliot deduces as follows : **"The unity of race of all these peoples, their community of origin, becomes then indisputable, and it is clearly from the vast plains that stretch along the base of the Himalayas that the white race had their origin."**

The same author further says, "Adopting this conclusion, the fabulous halo that surrounds the cradle of antiquity, on which history is reduced to conjectures void of foundation, explains itself, and it becomes possible to clear up the obscurity of the past."

On the basis of the comparison of Greek names with

those of Sanskrit Louis Jacolliot observes the Indian roots of Greece as follows:

> **From the several comparisons that I have made, it comes out that all the heroes of ancient Greece, and all the exploits that made them illustrious, are but souvenirs of India preserved and transmitted by poetry and tradition, and, later, their Indian origin lost sight of, and their primitive language transformed; sung and celebrated afresh by the first Greek poets, as pertaining to the origin of their own proper history.**

The Olympus of the Greeks is but a reproduction of the Indian Olympus. The legend of Jason and the Golden Fleeces is still in every mouth on the soil of India; and **the Iliad of Homer is nothing but an echo, and enfeebled souvenir of the Rāmāyaṇa**. An Indian Epic poem in which Rāma goes at the head of his allies to recover his wife, Sītā, who had been carried of by the King of an island on Laṅkā (0^0 longitude).

The chiefs insult each other in the same style, combat on cars, with lance and javelin. This struggle, in like manner, divides gods and goddesses; these take part with the king of Laṅkā, those with Rāma; – not even the wrath of Achilles at the loss of Briseis, but may be identified in this immense poem.

The imitation is flagrant, undeniable, met with even in details. The epithet Boopis (ox-eyed), which Homer constantly applies to Juno, is to the Indian the most sublime of comparisons; because, without however being adored as a god the ox is the animal especially revered in the Indian creed, and the epithet is wholly inexplicable in Greek.

Needles to say, that on Homer I entirely concur in the opinion of learned Germans, who consider the works of this poet as a succession of chants or rhapsodies, preserved by tradition and collected and arranged under

Pericles. It is the only conclusion that accords with the genius of new peoples, and especially of people of Indian origin.

With ancient fabulists the imitation is still more striking, and we may say, without fear of being taxed with exaggeration, that Æsop and Babrias have but copied Indian fable the reached them through Persia, Syria and Egypt. This latter writer, although a Greek himself, takes care at the commencement of his second proem to claim for the East the merit of inventing these ingenious apologues, which under an amusing form often suggest profound instruction.

Fable, O son of King Alexander, is an ancient invention of Syrian men, who lived in former times under Ninus and Belus.

It is sufficient to open the fables of the Indian Pilpay, of the Brahmin Ramsamyayer, of Aesop, of Babrias and La Fontaine, to see that they all proceed the one from the other, and that the Greek and modern fabulists have not even given themselves the trouble to change the action of these little dramas.

Thus, at each step and the more we study the ancients the more obvious appears the proposition I have already advanced, viz., that antiquity had itself an antiquity that inspired and aided its rapid advancement to that high degree of civilisation, artistic, philosophic and literary, which in its turn has fertilised modern genius.

How many wonderful facts" wrote M. Langlois, the translator of *Harivaṁśa*, "we have to learn of others.

And yet Governments exhaust themselves in excavations in scientific missions to Egypt, Persia, Africa, and the learned build clever systems on broken columns and inscriptions! Of course this is not without use, and we have made great progress in knowledge of the past, but the links of the chain are too interrupted to admit of reconstruction. **Why not send to India to explore origins and translate books? It is there alone the truth will be found.**

Wherefore continue to cultivate this school of Athens, which has no longer a raison d'etre, can no longer afford the faintest service; instead of replacing it by a Sanskrit school, which, founded at Pondicherry or Karikal, in the South of India, would render important services to science?

Dr. Ravi Prakash Arya
1051, Sector-1, Rohtak-124001
Haryana, India
9.4.2005 Ph. +91 9313033917
vedicscience@rediffmail.com
vedicscience@hotmail.com
vedicscience@gmail.com
www.vedicscience.net

II

Indian Tradition of Marriage Reached Europe

In support of the theory that India has given civilisation to the world, we shall now rapidly expose the most salient points of Indian legislation – legislation which we recover entire at Rome, bequeathed to her by Greece and Egypt, by them derived from primitive sources.

Obviously we can here only give some succinct hints; our whole volume would be insufficient to elaborate the subject.

In all social systems the most important matters of legislation are marriage, foliation, paternal authority, tutelage, adoption, property, the laws of contract, deposit, loan, sale, partnerships, donations, and testaments.

In the words of Louis Jacolliot, "We shall see, on examination, that these divisions have passed almost unaltered, from Indian law into Roman law and French law, and that the greater part of their particular dispositions are to-day still in vigour. There can be no comment or possible discussion; where there is a text there is no room for dissent."

According to Louis Jacolliot, "The Indian laws were codified by Manu, more than three thousand years before the Christian era, copied by entire antiquity and notably by Rome, which alone has left us written law – the code of Justinian, which has been adopted as the base of all modern legislation."

He makes a lengthy comparison of Indian and Roman

Laws proving his thesis by evidences in the following pages. Accordingly,

> Marriage, by the Indian law, is accomplished by the giving of the woman by the father and her acceptance by the husband, with the ceremony of water and fire.

> The same form at Rome (Leg. 66.i Digest of Justinian). Virgini in hortos, deductæ . . . Die nuptiarum priusquam ad eum transiret, et priusquam aqua et igne acciperetur, id est nuptie celebrarentur . . . obtulit decem aureos dono.

> The union of hands, as well as the confarreatio (or eating the bride-cake), of the Roman rite, are but copies of ordinances of Manu.

> In Indian marriage two different epochs are to be considered ---- the betrothal and the celebration; the betrothal always takes place some years before the final ceremony.

> The same usage, the same distinct periods, relegated to Rome.

> The word betrothal (*sponsalia*) Leg.2, tit. i. 1.23. of the Digest, comes from the word to promise (a *spondendo*), for it was a custom of the ancients to stipulate for the promise of a future wife.

> "Often," says law 17, under the same head, "sufficient cause may prolong the period of betrothal not only for one or two, but even for three, four, or more years."

> The consent by contract required by Hindu law was also required at Rome – Law 2, clause ii, *sponsalia sicut nuptia consensu contrahentium fiunt.*

> With the Hindu the young wife remains with her family until the age of puberty; the father then sends a message to the husband to intimate that his rights have commenced, and that he may claim his wife.

The same at Rome : *In potestate manente filia, pater sponse nuntium remittere potest.* -- (Leg. I0, *de Sponsalibus.*)

Conducting the wife to the house of her husband, was in India, as in Rome, the final ceremony of marriage – and was celebrated with music and feasting.

Marriages, by the law of Manu are prohibited of every degree in the direct line; and, in the collateral, to the seventh degree on the paternal, and fifth degree of the maternal line. Lastly, thc father, who in India marries his daughter to any one, after having betrothed her to another, is held infamous.

Listen to the Roman law (Leg. I3, §1. lib. iii): *Item st alteri sponsa, alteri nupta sit ex sententia edicti punitur.*

This is not all. The Hindu spirit is found to govern Roman law, even in those liaisons which modern legislation, except that of Brazil, has declined to recognise. Concubinage, tolerated and regulated at Rome, is another Indian institution which went to Rome in deference to tradition: the strict and pure manner of primitive times would never have inspired the sanction of licentious love.

We do but touch here upon all these points of interest. What important critical studies might not a deeper exploration afford us of those admirable laws of the ancient cradle of humanity!

Louis Jacolliot cites one more comparison. Accordingly, "A divorce, legally instituted in India, was the same in Rome. She cites from the Hindu legislator the causes for which a woman may separate from her husband."

According to Hindu law, "The husband may be abandoned by his wife if he is criminal, impotent, degraded, afflicted with leprosy, or because of a prolonged absence in foreign countries."

The Roman law, according to Jacolliot, states no other causes : degradation civil death, impotence, contagious disease, and absence.

In India, as in Rome, the adulterous wife loses her dowry. The husband is not obliged to restore it.

"Thus" says Jacolliot, "in this very important part of law, which is the base of societies and of nations, we see India giving lessons by which all peoples have profited. Let us pursue these comparisons, which although summary, are neither less sure nor less authentic."

III

Indian Laws forms the Basis of European Laws

It is important to note here that Indian laws on filiation, Paternal Authority, Tutelage, and Adoption forms the basis of European laws. Louis Jacolliot an expert on the legal matters on India as well as Europe could make an interesting comparison of Indian and European rules. Accordingly, the rule, *Pater is est quem justa nuptiae demonstrant,* admitted as an axiom in Roman law, and adopted by our code thus expressed in Article 312, "The child conceived during marriage, has the husband as father," is thus expressed by Manu.

"The child born in a house belongs to the husband of the woman."

She finds that the Hindu law distinguishes children as legitimate and natural, incestuous and adulterous. Natural children have a right, though a small one, in the succession of their parents. The children of incest or adultery can claim nothing but aliment.

It then establishes the procedure for repudiation, in these terms: "If from circumstances it is proven with certainty that the real father is some other than the husband, the child is the adulterous, and deprived of all rights in the family." Lastly, a very remarkable disposition is, that it admits the legitimatisation of natural child by subsequent marriage of the parents. On this issue Jacolliot Observes :

"We may say, without fear of error, that all the above principles, adopted by the Roman law, still form the substance of the laws of France and of the

majority of European nations. What admiration must fill the thinker, the philosopher, the jusriscounsult at sight of legislation so wise, so simple, so practical, that even after five thousand years we could not, find superior to supplant inherited Indian Laws."

Jacolliot finds a startling coincidence in India and Rome in the matter of filiation, paternal authority. He observes as follows :

The head of a family, says Gibelin, held his wife, his children, his slaves in his hand by the right of master, and with the same power; even to-day the son can acquire nothing, possess nothing that is not his father's.

Whatever his age, says the Indian commentator Kātyāyana, while his father is in life the son is never independent.

As to tutelage, the principles are always the same as admitted and now recognised in the Roman law. It would seem, in truth, that instead of studying India we are in reality upon modern soil.

Hindu law admits the legal tutelage, first of progenitors, next of paternal and maternal relations, and lastly dative, guardianship, as well as the intervention of a family council and of public authority for protection of the person and property of a minor.

It may be noted as a special coincidence, that the Hindu legislator prefers male to female tutelage, as long as male relative exist. A still more striking accordance is that the mother forfeits the tutelage of her children, if, being a widow, she marries again without consent of a family council.

We may conclude our glance at Indian law on this point with a word on adoption. The Hindu code permits adoption whether to introduce a child into a childless family, or from motives of good-will towards the adopted himself. As in Roman law, the adoption should be solemnised in presence of the family, of patriarchs, Brahmins, and heads of caste.

French law, in adopting the usage, has sought to give extraordinary solemnity and authenticity to the act in requiring that its adoption shall only be permitted after consent of a tribunal of first instance and of a superior court.

Once adopted the child became one of the family, with the same right as children who might afterwards be born. The same disposition are in Roman and French law.

Here for the Indian view Jacolliot refers to Vriddha Gautama as annotated by Nanda Pandita. It says, "If there exist an adopted son, of good disposition, and a legitimate son born afterwards, let them equally share the secession of their father."

Greek Law of Adoption Borrowed from Manu

According to Jacolliot, at Athens the formula of adoption was :

I adopt that I may have a son to accomplish on my tomb the sacred ceremonies, to perpetuate my race, and in transmitting my name through an unbroken chain of descendants, confer upon it some degree of immortality.

She finds this Greek formula of adoption, a reproduction of the Indian text of Manu?

I, who am without male descendants, hasten with solicitude to adopt a son for the continuation of funeral offerings and sacred rites, and for the perpetuation of my name.

She further remarks, in conclusion, that the Indian law was the first to consider marriage as an indissoluble bond.

Even death did not dissolve it, for in the castes that permitted re-marriage of widows, it was only in cases where the defunct having left no children, it became imperative to provide for him a son, who should accomplish on his tomb the ceremonies necessary for his salvation. For, in Hindu theology, the father can only attain the abodes of the blessed through the expiatory ceremonies of his son. The second husband, therefore, was only permitted as a means, the child begotten by him was not his, but belonged to and inherited the property of the defunct.

Jacolliot is appreciative of the respectful place given to women by Indian scriptures. She observes :

> Besides, what antiquity wholly overlooked, but what we cannot too much admire in India, is its respect for women, almost amounting to a worship.

> This extract from Manu (lib. 3, *śloka* 55 etc.) will not be read without surprise:

> "Women should be nurtured with every tenderness and attention by their fathers, their brothers, their husbands, and their brothers-in-law, if they desire great prosperity."

> "Where women live in affliction, the family soon becomes extinct; but when they are loved and respected, and cherished with tenderness, the family grows and prospers in all circumstances."

> "When women are honoured, the divinities are content; but when we honour them not, all acts of piety are sterile."

> *yatra nāryastu pūjyante, ramante tatra devatā.*

> "The households cursed by the women to whom they have not rendered due homage, find ruin weigh them

down and destroy them as if smitten by some secret power."

"In the family where the husband is content with his wife, and the wife with her husband, happiness is assured forever."

This veneration of woman produced in India an epoch of adventurous chivalry, during which we find the heroes of Indian poem accomplishing high deeds, which reduce all the exploits of the Amadis, Knights of the Round Table, and the Paladins of the Middle Age, to mere child's play.

Grand and peaceful epoch! Which India has, to-day, some-what forgotten. But whose the fault, if not those brutal and stupid invasions, which for ages dispute her fine and fertile soil?

Indian Laws of Property Shapes the European Laws

(Laws of Property, contract, Deposit, Loan, Sale, Partnership, Donation, And Testamentary Bequest)

According to Louis Jacolliot : "The Indian laws of property are not less admirable then those of the person; they proceed with a largeness of view and justness of discrimination, unsurpassed by successive modern legislation. Those laws, collected by Rome, are still, with little alteration, our own French Laws." She further elaborates her arguments as follows :

Jurisconsults, of our times, are divided, on the origin of property, between two systems: the first admit the right of property only as based upon natural law, and would, consequently, reduce it to possession; the others consider it as a social necessity, and derive it from legal enactment.

This Indian legislator who proposes to himself the same

question, thus resolves it - Where occupation shall be proven, but where no kind of title shall appear, sale cannot be admitted. A title, and not occupation, is essential to proprietorship.-- (Manu, lib. viii., śl. 200.)

Such the principle proprietorship in India then derived from law. It is the same idea that pervades the entire economy of European Codes.

Passing, then, to the manner of acquiring things that as yet belong to no one, or, as from their nature, have but an accidental owner, Manu declares that, "the field cultivated is the property of him who cleared it of wood, and the gazelle, of the first hunter that mortally wounded it.

Examining in course the nature of property in itself, the Indian law divides it into movable and immovable, -- a distinction which modern legislators have adopted without change, but which was rejected by the Roman law.

Immovables are themselves divided into immovables from their nature, and immovables from their destination; then possessions, in connection with those who hold them, are classed as belonging to no individual and as belonging to all, -- as public and as private property. The Indian law decrees the latter alone to be subject to commercial transactions between individuals.

"Thus all classifications of properties," says Gibelin, "according to their nature, their source, their tenure, and, lastly, the rights of proprietorship, are, in Europe, so many traditions of Indian legislation adopted into existing French law, as into Roman law; provision for the family, the adjustment of disposable quotas, contracts not only in their essence, but also in their application; in fact, all those principles which civil law has reduced to the most simple expression, by fusion of Roman law with German usage; that is, by reunion of the double traditions of the Indian tribes who came to people the North and the South; on the one side, by Russia, the Scandinavian countries, and Germany, and, on the other, by Persia, Egypt, Greece and Rome.

In India, all transfer of property, by whatever title effected, conditional or gratuitous, was to be accomplished with the forms of donation; that is, by delivery of gold and water – with corn and grass – *tila et cuse.*

The gold was presented by the vendor or donor to the purchaser or receiver, to ensure his satisfaction, should the property prove of insufficient value. The water was spilled, as at a marriage, in sign of gift; the corn and grass were presented as part and produce of the property, in sign of transfer.

And here in France, we may no doubt, were learned all the various formulas of solemnising contracts, as well as the northern customs of transfer by water and earth, by herb and branch. On all these points, we are constrained to recognise the influence of Indian law.

We shall be still more brief in our few remaining glances at Indian legislation, for, taken together, we have already said enough to justify the conclusions we pretend to draw from this summary *expose* of the Sanskrit origin and general principles of Hindu jurisprudence.

A few words, however, on contracts, donations, and wills, may, perhaps, not be ill-received by the reader; in fact, the different modes of engagement, and of donations between the living or because of death, are in a manner still more striking, if possible, copied in their principles and in their effects, both by the Roman law and by modern legislators.

As the first principle necessary to the validity of

engagements, the ancient Indian legislator indicates the competence of the parties.

Women in the power of husbands, children, slaves, and those under interdict, are incompetent.

The incapacity absolute for children and slaves; relative for the woman, who may contract with the authority of her husband, and for the interdicted, whom the prohibition simply subjects to the authority of his tutor.

Observe, *en passant,* this striking coincidence with French law, that the Hindu wife, in default of her husband's authority, may release herself from her incapacity, by authority of justice.

Besides these incapacity which may terminate by a change of condition, the majority of the minor, or the emancipation of the slave, for instance, the law establishes others founded on a particular situation of persons. – (*Digest of Hindu Laws,* vol. ii. p. 193, and Manu).

The contact made by a man who is drunk, foolish, imbecile, or grievously disordered in his mental condition, by an old man whose weakness is abused, and by all persons without power, is entirely void.

Manu further adds, "What is held under compulsion-- held by force-- is declared null."

Would not this be thought a mere commentary on the Code Napoleon of four or five thousand years after?

How far is all this from those barbarous customs of first ages, when every question was solved by violence and force; and what admiration should we not feel for a people who, at the epoch at which Biblical fable would date the world's creation, had already reached the extraordinary degree of civilisation indicated by laws so simple and so practical!

Let us not delude ourselves: the best criterion of the

condition of nations is their written law.

We shall not now enter into the minutae of contracts which would be perfectly understood in their details and consequences only by persons connected with law. Referring such readers to the sources themselves, it is sufficient for us to state that guarantee, **salary, pledge, rent, lease, hypothecation, and mortgage with usufructs, wholly of Indian origin, have passed successively into Roman and French law entire, and without other modification than such as necessarily result to nations from the predominance of civil over religious law.**

Still more, if we descended into details, should we see that all the pleas recognised by Roman and French laws for the extinction of obligations had been foreseen and applied by Indian legislation.

So, mutation, remission of the debt, cession of property, compensation, the loss of the thing due in specified cases, actions to annual or rescind, by possessor or claimant, are admitted in India, and have the same effect as with us.

To whom the merit of priority? That, I think, cannot be questioned.

Listen to the text of *Smṛti-Chandrikā*, authorising substitution, "The creditor may transfer, either to his own creditor or to a third person who releases him, the pledge delivered by his debtor in surety of debt, with the voucher that establishes it, but in making mention that he, the debtor, consents to all these circumstances of the transfer."

And this other formal text from the same work on tender and consignation, "If the creditor refuse to receive his credit when tendered in payment by the debtor, let the amount of his debt, fruit, money, merchandise or cattle, be deposited by the latter to that effect, in the hands of a third person, and the interest shall cease to accrue as soon as the deposit is effected."

This procedure affords acquittal.

According to Louis Jacolliot, "To give an idea of the interesting work of comparison to which a jurisconsult might devote himself, and still more to demonstrate in a manner more evident, that the laws of Rome, as well as our own, are but a copy of antique Indian jurisprudence."

She collates, as per Gibelin, texts of the three legislations on deposit, loan at usury or interest, or without interest.

Indian text: *Kātyāyana Smṛti* –"What is lent from good-will bears no interest."

Civil code, Art. I876. – "A loan of convenience is essentially gratuitous."

Roman Law.--"Commodata restunc proprie intelligitur, si nulla mercede accepta vel constituta, res tibi utenda data est."

Indian Text : *Kātyāyana Smṛti* – "If the thing perish by its own vice, the borrower is not responsible, unless there is fault on his part."

Civil Code, Art. I884 – "If the thing deteriorates from the sole effect of the usage for which it is borrowed, and without any fault of the borrower, he is not answerable for the deterioration."

Roman Law – "Quod vero senectute contigit, vel morbo, vel vi latronum ereptum est, aut quid simile accidit, dicendum est nihil eorum esse imputandum ei qui commodatum accipit, nisi aliqua culpa interveniat."

Indian Text : Kātāyana "When a thing lent on usage for a definite time is reclaimed before the term or accomplishment of the said usage, the borrower cannot be forced to restore it."

Civil Code, Art. I888 – "The lender cannot withdraw the thing lent before the covenanted term, or in default of convention, until after it has served the purpose for which it was borrowed"

Roman Law – "Adjuvari quippe nos, non decipi beneficio oportet."

Indian Text : *Kātāyana Smṛti* – "But where the interests of the owner may be compromised by an urgent need of the thing lent, the borrower may be forced to restore it even before the stipulated time."

Civil Code, Art. I889 – "Nevertheless, if in the interval, or before the borrower's need is over, an urgent and unforeseen want of the thing should come upon the lender, the judge can, according to circumstances, oblige the borrower to return it to him."

Indian Text : *Nārada Smṛti* – "When a man, in confidence, entrusts his effects to another, on condition of restitution, it is an act of deposit."

Civil Code, Art. I915 – "Deposit in general is an act by which we receive the property of another, in charge to preserve, and to restore it as received."

Roman Law, – "Depositum et quod custodendum alicui datum est."

Indian Text : – *Vṛhaspati Smṛti* "The depository who allows the thing deposited to be destroyed by his negligence, while preserving his own property with a care altogether different, will be forced to pay its value with interest."

Civil Code, Art I927– "The depository shall bestow on preservation of the things deposited the same care as he bestows on the preservation or things belonging to himself."

Roman Law – "Nec enim salva fide minorem iis quam suis rebus diligentiam praestabit."

Indian Text : *Yājñvalkya Smṛti* – "The depository will not restore what has been destroyed by the King by Providence or by thieves. But if this loss follows after his refusal of restitution on demand, he shall return the value of the deposit, and pay a fine of equal amount."

Civil Code, Art. I929 – "The depository is not liable in any case for accidents from superior force, unless he has made a delay in returning the thing deposited."

Roman Law – "Si depositum quoque, eo die depositi acutm sit periculo ejus, apud quem depositum furit, est si judicii accipiendi tempore potuit, id reddere reus, nec reddidit."

Indian Text, *Id* – "If the trustee use the trust without consent of the proprietor, he shall be punished and forced to pay the price of the things deposited with interest."

Civil Code, Art. I930 – "He may not make use of the thing deposited without the permission expressed or understood of the depositor."

Roman Code – "Qui rem depositam, invito domino, sciens prudensque, in usus convertit, etiam furti delicto succedit."

Indian Text: *Id* – "What is enclosed in a box deposited in the hands of a trustee without any declaration of its contents, should be unknown, and so restored.

Civil Code, Art. I93I – "He should not seek to know the things that have been deposited, if they have been confided to him in a closed box or under a sealed envelope."

On the Same question, Manu further says:

"In the case of sealed deposit, the trustee who would escape censure, should restore it to the depositor without changing the seal."

Indian Text: *Manu* – "The deposit shall be restored as received, both in quality and quantity."

Civil Code, Art. I932 – "The depository should restored identically the thing deposited."

Indian Text: *Manu Smṛti* – "If the deposit is seized by thieves, attacked by vermin, carried away by water, or consumed by fire, the depository is not liable for its restoration, unless the loss or deterioration is the result of this act."

Civil Code, Art. I933 – "The trustee is only bound to restore the thing deposited in the condition in which it may be found at the moment of restitution. Deterioration, which have not occurred from his fault, are at the charge of the depositor,"

Roman Code – "Quod vero senectute contigit, vel morbo, vel vi latronum ereptum est, nihil eorum esse imputandum nisi aliqua culpa interveniat."

Indian Text : *Bṛhaspati Smṛti* – "Whatever profit the depository may derive from the object deposited he should restore with it."

Civil Code, Art. I936 – "If the thing deposited has produced profit that have been received by the depository, he is obliged to restore them."

Roman Law – "Hanc actionem bonæ fidei esse dubitari non oportet Et ideo, et fructus in hanc actionem venire, et omnem causam, et partan. Disendum est ne nuda res veniat."

Indian Text : *Manu Smṛti* – "The thing deposited should be restored to him who deposited it."

Civil Code, Art. 1837 – "The depository should not restore the thing deposited, except to the person who confided it to him."

Indian Text : *Manu Smṛti* – "The trustee cannot be

arraigned by any one when he restores the deposit to the heir of a dead depositor."

Civil Code, Art. I939 – "In case of the natural or civil death of the depositor, the thing deposited may only be given up to his heir."

Indian Text : *Manu Smṛti* – "In the place where the deposit was delivered, there must it be restored.

Civil Code Art. I943 – "If the contract names no place of restitution. It should be made at the place of deposit."

Indian Text : *Bṛhaspati* – "Let the trustee guard the deposit with care, and restore it on the first demand of the depositor."

Civil Code, Art. I943 – "The deposit should be restored to the depositor whenever he reclaims it."

Roman Code – Est autem apud Julianum ... scriptum, eum qui rem deposuit, statim posse depositi actionem agere. Hoc enim ipso dolo facere eum qui suscepit quod reposcenti rem non dat."

Indian Text : *Manu Smṛti* – "He who does not restore a deposit after having received it, is declared infamous by the law."

Civil Code, Art. I945– "The unfaithful depository is not admitted to the benefit of acquittance."

Is it necessary longer to continue these studies and comparisons, and is it possible to make demonstration more clear, especially if we bear in mind the ages that separate us from this epoch, and the necessary transformations that all these things have undergone?

These approximations might be made throughout all jurisprudence; we should constantly find Indian legislation rational, philosophic, complete, and worthy on all points to give birth to the written law

of the world.

Sale, donations, testaments of which we have seen the general principles, would present us the same logical filiation in detail, the same points of contract, the same basis, enlightened by the strictest good sense.

Source of all modern laws on matter, scarce, here and there some few changes, which attach to difference of manners, climate, civilisation, and but serve better to demonstrate the connection; for ancient and modern legislation only they depart from those of India, where new mattes have imperatively exacted other laws.

The legislator Manu, whose authenticity is incontestable, dates back more than three thousand years before the Christian era; the Indian Scholars assign him a still more ancient epoch.

Indian Chronology More in Harmony with Science

Louis Jacolliot finds here Indian chronology more in harmony with science than the Biblical one. On this issue he observes as follows :

What instruction for us, and what testimony almost material in favour of the Oriental chronology, which, less ridiculous than ours (Indian Chronology more in harmony with secure based on Biblical traditions), adopts, for the formation of this world, an epoch more in harmony with science!

We are no longer of the times to incur risk of stake and fagot for contradicting a text of the Bible or of Aristotle. But we should recollect that the regime of the middle ages has bequeathed us an innumerable assemblage of opinions and ready made ideas, from which we have the greatest difficulty in disembarrassing ourselves.

In vain science, at first timidly, then boldly, has made

itself the demolisher of all these prejudices, its advance is slow; and as the grown man never succeeds in completely forgetting the tales that have amused his cradle – so are western nations incapable of rejecting certain fables of past ages, as, it must be confessed, they are equally incapable of believing them.

There are certain ideas discussed freely in society, which we should blush to believe on conscientious examination; for when alone with himself, man always exacts serious reasons for his convictions.

If agitated or discussed in public, a hundred voices rise to cry, haro, "That must not be touched!" is heard from all sides And wherefore? Respect this, respect that! Again, wherefore? We have a love for old things, and it revolts us to change our old habits.

If, for example, one should happen to say that the chronology that assigns to the world's creation a date of only six thousand years(Usher's dating of creation of Earth as 4004 BCE), is absurd nonsense, what tempests would he not raise in certain camps, and, the knife at his throat, he must give mathematical reasons, while they think it right to oppose only fables and sacred texts!

Let us release ourselves from all this load of timid credulities, and we shall then comprehend that it docs not belong to us Western people, the last-comers, proudly to fix the origin of the world by the light of souvenirs of yesterday's birth, and thus, by a stroke of the pen, to erase the civilisation and history of the Indian people who have preceded us by many thousands of years upon earth. More logical than ourselves, these people, who might have been content with their antiquity, professed themselves the issue of other peoples who had preceded them, and who had become extinct from a series of cataclysms similar to that of which all

existing notions retain a souvenir.

Be it as it may, we are constrained to admit, in considering these admirable laws, organising society, the family, property, exhibiting, in a word, the most advanced civilisation, that this progress could no more have been accomplished in a day by the Hindus than by ourselves, and that ages would be required to realise it.

A few brace of centuries led ancient and modern nations to this condition, thanks to the Asiatic light that came to direct, and abridge for them the period of gestation. But how much longer must that period have been for Indians even in admitting their opinions, that they too had precursors to light their coming way?

The more I advance in these comparative studies, the more obvious does it became that all peoples and civilisations proceed as fatally from preceding peoples, as do sons from fathers, as the inferior links of chain hang from the superior links; and that however obscure may be this filiation, those ties which connect them, it is easy, with the aid of patient and unprejudiced research, to re-attach them the one to the other.

There is, certainly, here no new idea of which to claim the merit. Modern history has already guessed its cradle and struggles against those mediaeval legacies which, in controlling thought, have so long retarded the advance of intelligence towards a more free and more rational comprehension of the past.

Commenting on the chronology of Indian philosophy and religion, which alike rest upon the Vedas, he observes as follows :

In point of authenticity, the Vedas have incontestable precedence over the most ancient records. These holy books which, according to the Vedic Indian tradition, contain the revealed word of God, were honoured in India long before Persia, Asia Minor, Egypt, and

Europe, were colonised or inhabited by Indians.

"We cannot refuse to the Vedas", says celebrated Orientalist, Sir William Jones, "the honour of an antiquity the most distant". But, at what epoch were they composed? Who their author? We may revert to times the most primitive, interrogate the most ancient records of the human race, and it is still impossible to solve these questions; all are silent on the subject. Some authors retroject their composition to the first periods after the Cataclysm; but, according to the Vedic Indian tradition they are anterior to creation; they were, says the *Sāmaveda* formed of the soul of him who exists by, or of himself.

The Vedas are four in number : the *Ṛgveda*, *Sāmaveda*, *Yajurveda*, and *Atharvaveda*. Only a few fragments of these books have been translated and made known to the learned word; ere long an English translation, due to the labours of the Calcutta Asiatic Society, will permit their collected study.

Indian philosophy is divided into orthodox and heterodox system.

Among the most celebrated authors of orthodox philosophy , Vyāsa appear in first rank – the latter commonly known under the name of Kṛṣṇa Dvaipāyana Veda Vyāsa, because he is said to have compiled the mantras of the four Vedas.

Jaiminī was of Saṁnyāsī or mendicant class, clothed in yellow and carrying staff and bowl. Vyāsa it appears sacrificed more to things of this world, and enjoyed in India a reputation as poet, at least equal to that of philosopher. Sir W. Jones speaks of him with veneration.

The works of these two authors who have sustained the scholastic philosophy of India are known; that of Jaiminī under the name of *Pūrva-Mimānsā*; and that of

Vyāsa, under the title of *Uttra-Mimānsā*, or *Vedānta*.

Their object is not only to comment upon the Vedas, and determine their meaning, but Jaiminī also treats of casuistry; and the work of Vyāsa contains a *dialectique* in the manner of Aristotle, with a psychology where the author pushes scepticism and idealism to the point of denying the existence of a material world.

It is the system of Pyrrho entire. Without doubt, this philosopher, who had travelled in India, had from intercourse with Indian scholars, brought back this principle, that all is illusion – save only God himself.

The *Pūrva-Mimānsā* exhibits, besides, a great affinity with the mysterious dogma of the philosopher of Samos, which Plato had, in fact, adopted.

According to Jaiminī, all is harmony in the universe, all a perpetual concert; God himself is a harmonious sound, and all the beings he has created are but modifications of his premier-ship.

From this system of sounds naturally flows that of numbers, to which the *Mimānsā* attributes a mysterious power. The numbers one and three are the symbol of the Trinity, in unity, the sign of the three attributes of the Divinity-creation, preservation, and transformation by destruction.

It is in the same sense that the priest of Memphis, in Egypt, explained the number three to the novice, by intimating that the Premier Monad created to Dyad, who engendered the Triad, and that it is this Triad that shines throughout Nature.

The number two expresses androgynous Nature, the active and the passive, the generating power, base of all sacred legends, source whence mythographers have extracted their immense variety of fables; of symbols, and of ceremonies.

"When Manu says - "The Sovereign Power Divine had finished the work of Creation, he was absorbed in the spirit of God, and thus exchanged his period of energy for a period of repose." We shall, later, occupy ourselves more specially with this idea of the Trinity, and indicate whence acquired by all religions, without distinction.

The authors of the two *Mimānsās* have equally treated on questions the most abstract, the efficacy of works (*Karma*); Grace (*Iśvara-Prasāda*); Faith (*Śraddhā*); and freedom of judgement; and raised the question of the nominalists and realists, long before Abeilard and William de Champeaux.

This was in India the epoch of fervent faith, the epoch when all science, philosophy, and morale were sought in a text of Holy Scripture.

Of the Śastras and the *Mahābhārata*, which profess the same doctrines, the dates are lost in the night of time. If we are to accept the chronology of Vedic tradition, as calculated by the learned Orientalist Halhed, they must possess, the first an antiquity of seven *Manvantaras* (of 30 Million duration each), and the second of four millions of years (*Mahāyuga* System) – a chronology which strikes point blank at all our European ideas on matter.

Such things easily excite laughter, especially in France, the country to superficial spirits and of inconsiderate affirmations. We have made a little world for ourselves, dating from scarce six thousand years, and created in six days; that satisfies all, and needs no thought.

Some, it is true, have of late, with the aid of science, tried to change these six days into six epochs. The margin is large, thousands of years may have slipped in between each epoch; this idea shakes hands with that of the East. But open wide your ears, and you will hear partisans of the past hurling from all sides denunciation against this advanced guard of elite, and bespattering it with their mud brooms.

Ah! Let us guard against ultramontanism, if we would not end, like the Hindus in demoralisation and stolidity.

The Śāstras are not the only works that claim such antiquity; according to philosophers, the laws of Manu were also established in the *Kṛta-Yuga*, or first age. The *Sūrya-Siddhānta* would retrodate many millions of years, and, on this subject, Halhed, the translator of the *Śāstras*, makes the remark, that no people possess annals of an authority so incontestable as those transmitted to us by the ancient Indian scholars and, in support of his assertion, mentions a book written more than four thousand years ago, which gives a retrospective history of the human race of many millions of years.

This chronology has nothing of exaggeration for Indians; on the contrary, it logically accords with their belief, which admits the existence of matter from all eternity with God.

What nation has conceived more ideas, agitated more questions, or discussed more problems? The development of thought, the progressive march of the science have taken nothing from the value of the philosophic speculation of those men, so far removed from us.

Legislation, *morale,* metaphysics, psychology, all have they penetrated -- fathomed all.

When we explore the monuments of Indian literature, when we open those vast philosophic magazines whence radiate, on all sides, the primordial lights that attest a high civilisation, we are struck with that majestic image of the Divinity, which poet, historian, legislator, and philosopher cease not to place before the eyes of men, in claiming their belief in his immediate

Providence."

It is not until after raising the spirit towards God, after offering to him the affectionate devotion of grateful hearts, that they proceed. The doctrine, the theories, the sublime conceptions of these sages, lead us to a most profound admiration for their faith and their belief.

"The Ganges that flows," says the *Sāmaveda*, "it is God, the sea that roars, it is him; the wind that blows, it is him; the cloud that thunders, the lightning's flash, it is him; as from all eternity the world was in the spirit of Brahman, so to-day all that exists is His image.

Manu, before inviting Bhṛgu to reveal to his disciples, the Mahārcas as his immortal laws, begins by explaining to them the attributes of the Divinity, and the mysteries of Creation. In the same way, the author of the *Mahābhārata* unveils, in majestic language, by the mouth of the Divine son of Devakī to the astonished Arjuna, all the sublime ideas of Vedic Deism. And the Śāstras, of which we have above spoken, lead the reader at once to a knowledge of the superior Intelligence who created all, arranged all, with power infinite and uncontrolled.

But after these first ages of fervent faith, of belief without question, soon came the worship of pure reason, which, without rejecting ancient revelation, would only admit it purified by freedom of judgement.

The liberty necessarily beget the most diverse systems; side by side with the spiritualists appeared the sceptics, whose theories were revived by the ancient Pyrrhoniens, and in our own days, by the disciples of Montaigne and of Kant without the merit on the part of these latter, of a single additional argument.

The Sāṅkhya philosophy, whose founder was Kapila also maintains that the existence of a spiritual element cause the birth of the universe; further, that it is, neither demonstrated by the senses, nor by reasoning, that is, neither by perception, nor by induction, two of the tree criteria of truth, by which according to it we arrive at a knowledge of things. For the nature of the cause and of the effect being the same, it results that which does not exist cannot, by any possible operation of a cause, receive existence.

An argument analogous to that employed by Leucippus, Lu cretius, etc., that to create, God must construct the world out of naught, and that it is not possible to extract something from nothing.

Yet, Kapila recognised a plastic force inherent in nature, a being proceeding from her, special attribute of matter, and the source of all individual intelligence.

From the opposing action of the creative quality and the destructive quality proceeds operative force, or movement, which itself possesses three distinctive qualities: 1st, the plastic; 2nd the repulsive; 3rd, the inert.

Such the subtleties in which the play of Indian imagination indulged in those early times.

Indian philosopher are very elaborate in examination of these three qualities, or inseparable attributes, of Nature, and which intrinsically permeate all that exists. They are not mere accidents of Nature, says Gautama, in his Treatise of Philosophy, but they form its essence and enter into its composition.

The first is the presence of all that is good, and the absence of all that is evil.

The last is the absence of all that is good, and the presence of all that is evil.

The middle quality partakes of the two others.

Let us remark that the doctrine of the Śāstras most surprisingly resembles the system of many philosophers of antiquity. Empedocles admitted, as the principle of things, four elements; but he at the same time recognised the principle of concord and the principle of discord.

Plato taught that Love was the most powerful of the Gods, the true creator, and that he was born of Chaos.

The Stoics had recourse to a unique substance producing the four elements, and the philosopher of Stagyara admitted a fifth, to which he assigned the origin of the soul.

Energy or mobility, according to the *Śāstras*, in alliance with time and goodness, engender matter, the great substance, the Maha-Buddha; and the shock of opposing currents in matter produced that subtle, celestial, luminous element called Agasa-a pure, electric, vivifying fluid diffused in space.

Thus affection is the universal mother, the first cause and supreme generatrix of the universe.

As spouse of Brahmā, quiescent, unrevealed, enveloped in darkness, as expressed in the *Mahābhārata*, it is Bhavānī.

As spouse of Brahma, passing from quiescence into action, animating matter, and manifesting himself by creation, it is Brāhmī.

As spouse of Viṣṇu, preserver and restorer, it is   Lakṣmī.

As spouse of Śiva, destroyer and reproducer, it is Pārvatī.

The Vedas consider Brahmā Puruṣa as having sacrificed himself for creation, to produce or create creation. Not only does God become incarnate and suffer for our regeneration and restoration, but He even immolated Himself to give us existence.

Brahmā is at once both *Ṛtvija* (performer) and *Yajamāna* (host) of *yajña*, so that the priest who officiates each morning at the ceremonies of the *Sarvamedha*, the universal *yajña*, symbolic of creation, in presenting his offering to God, identifies himself with the Divine performer of *yajña*, who is Brahmā. Or rather, it is Brahmā, born to His Son, Kṛṣṇa, who came to die on earth for our salvation, who Himself accomplishes the solemn sacrifice.

These last lines present points of curious and delicate comparison; but I will only touch upon this subject, with hands full of proof, in the chapter to be specially devoted to it, and that, with the impartiality of a free spirit that seeks only scientific truths, careless of the odium it may provoke.

When the Ruler of worlds saw the surface of the earth enamelled with exquisite flowers, the fields and meadows covered with vegetation, and Nature beaming with youth and vitality scatter all her treasures over the globe, He sent the Holy-Spirit, the Word, His First-begotten, who proceeded to the creation of animals and of man.

The God, say the Śāstras, presented himself provided with an infinite variety of forms and a multitude of organs-- striking image of that almighty power, that supreme wisdom, which no spirit can conceive, and of which no man has been able to measure the extent nor to fathom the depth.

To man he gave the five organs of touch, sight, smell taste, and hearing and a sixth, admitted by all Indian philosophers, and called *Manas*, which is the agent in union of the sexes.

The followers of Buddha, who was the reformer, the Luther of Brahminical theocratic authority, and whose doctrines spread over the north of Upper Asia, in Tartary, China, and even the Japan, recognised neither the sixth sense nor the fifth element. It is one of the many points on which they differ with the orthodox.

The *Sāṅkhya* philosophy thus defines it, "an organ by affinity, partaking the properties of others, and which serves it one for sensation and action."

We know that Aristotle also admitted the sixth sense.

The ancients were divided in opinion about the souls of Brutes: the Platonists accorded them reason and understanding, but in a less degree than man; the Peripatetic but allowed them sensation.

The *Śāstras* not only promise man immortality in heaven, but also loudly claim for animals immortality of soul and existence in a future life. Hence, without doubt, the doctrine of metempsychosis, which, from India where it was first conceived, spread to the rest of Asia and to Greece.

These works consider individual souls as emanations from the supreme soul of the universe, as a portion of the divine essence; – at the hour of decomposition they are reabsorbed into the bosom of God, as the rain-drop that falls upon the sand returns into the immense ocean, or, adopting the beautiful simile of the Vedas, "they are sparks that return to the immortal centre from which they were emitted."

Only the souls of those unsoiled in either heart or hand by sin or crime, meet and reunite, after shaking off mortality, with the divinity where the sentiment of individuality is lost in the general beatitude; while the guilty, after expiating their crimes in hell, undergo several migrations, and re-enter into the spiritual nature of Brahma only after being purified from their transgression.

The soul that returns to animate a new body, says the *Vedānta*, loses its first form, and, like the rain-drop that traverses the air to give strength and life to the plant on which it falls, it penetrates the embryo-animal that it comes to animate and vivify.

As we see, the eternity of punishment is a dogma which, as we think with reason, Indian philosophers do not admit; crime, whatever it be, apart from successive migrations, may and ought to be expiated by chastisement until the purified soul may be judged worthy of boundless felicity by reunion with the Great Whole, that "spreads undivided, operates unspent,"- the soul of the universe.

Faithful echo of Indian doctrines, Plato had the same ideas on the soul's destiny and the life to come; he considered it a ray from the supreme intelligence to which it should return, and the faculty of merging itself into the divinity was regarded by him as the reward of purity – which he denied to the impure.

We may conclude from this rapid sketch, that the traces of Indian philosophy which appear at each step in the doctrine professed by the illustrious men of Greece, abundantly prove that it was from the Indian came their science, and that many of them, no doubt, drank deeply at the primitive fountain.

It is possible more clearly to demonstrate the undeniable influence exercised by India over the rest of the world, and notably, on antiquity, by its language, its legislation, and its philosophy? It would, we think, require singularly robust and unintelligent powers of negation to dare maintain it. The face of such resemblance, I may say, of such *facsimiles,* that Greece and Rome owe nothing to India, and that they attained the civilisation which we know, by their own initiation, their own energy, and their own genius.

We readily admit that Rome was inspired by Greece, Greece by Asia-Minor and Egypt; why not, especially after the forcible proofs we have given, continue the same logical argument, and accept

India as the initiatrix of ancient peoples? There is in it neither paradox nor ingenious speculative theory, but merely a truth which is making its way, which all great Orientalists have long acknowledged, and which will, we think, be rejected only by men of certain party because too forcible an argument in favour of the identity of origin of the traditions and religious revelations of all peoples.

If India is truly the cradle of the white race, mother of different nations that occupy Asia, a part of Africa and Europe; in proof of this filiation we find, as well in antiquity as in modern times, the ineffaceable traces of this origin bequeathed us in her language, her legislation, her literature, her philosophic and moral science, does it not become evident that religious traditions, modified under the hand of time and the action of free thought, must have also come from India? For they are the recollections that emigrant people preserve most fondly, as holy ground between the new and the old country, where repose the ashes of those ancestors whom they shall see no more.

IV
Manes-Minos-Moses of West Originated from Manu of India

Manu was a great philosopher and first lawgiver of humankind who gave political and social institutions to India and the world.

The Egyptian legislator receives the name of Manes.

A Cretan visits Egypt to study the institutions with which he desired to endow his country, and history preserves his memory under the name of Minos.

Lastly, the liberator of the servile caste of Hebrews founds a new society and is named Moses. According to Louis Jacolliot :

Manu, Manes, Minos, Moses, -- these four names over-shadow the entire ancient world, they appear at the cradles of four different people to play the same role, surrounded by the same mysterious halo, all four legislators and high priests, all four founding theocratic and sacerdotal societies.

That they stood in the relation to each other of predecessor and successor, however distant, seems proven by similitude of name and identity of the institutions they created.

In Sanskrit Manu signifies the man par excellence, the legislator.

Manes, Minos, Moses, do they not betray an incontestable unity of derivation from the Sanskrit with the slight variations of different periods, and the different languages in which they are written-Egyptian, Greeks, and Hebrew?

We have here the clue that should guide our retrospective researches through all ancient civilisations, through all revelations and religious traditions to their true Indian sources, in those myths and fables of every kind that surround the infancy of most people, and which history has *piously* recorded and thus authenticated, instead of denouncing and relegating them to the domain of poetry and of fiction.

With such aid have the ambitious subjugated and ruled the people in ancient times; with the aid of such recollections is their subjugation sought to-day.

Manu was misinterpreted for their convenience by the mediaeval priests and Brahmins and became the starting point of the ruin and abasement of his country, stifled under a corrupt and egotistical theocracy.

His successor, Manes, in subjugating Egypt to priestly domination, prepared for its stagnation and oblivion.

And Moses, adopting with like success the despotic role of his precursors, could only make of his nation, so pompously proclaimed "The people of God!" a herd of slaves, well disciplined to the yoke, and constantly carried off into servitude by neighbouring populations.

A new era arose ----- but the purified religious idea of Christian philosophy becoming soon *sacerdotalised,* its inheritors issue from the catacombs to mount thrones, and from that moment apply themselves, without relaxation, to invert the master-principle, and to substitute for the sublime words.

"My kingdom is not of this world:" this other, which threatens to make its way,

"The entire world is our kingdom."

Let us beware; the times of Brahmanism, of Sacerdotalism, of Levitism, in India, in Egypt, in Judea, present nothing to compare with the flames of the

Inquisitions the Vandois massacres, or St. Bartholomew's, for which Rome made St. Peter's resound with a *Te Deum* of exultation!

Henry of Germany, Emperor and King, passing three days with his feet in the snow, his head bowed down under the vulgar hand of a fanatic priest, had no parallel midst votaries of Brahmā, of Isis, or of Jehovah. Let us beware!

1889 came to give the signal of struggle between those who would make God's law their guide to liberty and progress, and those who profess to avail themselves of the laws of God to destroy both progress and liberty.

No weakness! Let us look back, and see if we would desire to end like the nations of antiquity.

Let us foster the faith that thanks Gods for the reason he has given us. Let us spurn the faith that would make of God an instrument to subjugate reason."

V

European Classification of Society owes to India

Social institutions in the world are merely a contribution of India. Either they were inherited from Indian or designed on the basis of India by the migrators in the different parts of the world. The findings of Luis Jacolliot speak highly of this fact. Accordingly :

> Never did a civilisation exist so especially constructed to brave ages, and to survive invasions of every kind, as the Indian Society still in effective operation today, in spite of the loss of its ancient prestige and political power.

> Whence, then, came those persons who spoke a language the most beautiful and the most perfect, ---- who so penetrated, analysed, investigated in every form the problem, of life, as to leave nothing for innovation, either to antiquity or modern times, in the domain of literary, moral and philosophic sciences?--

> Whence came these men who, after having studied all, obscured all, reversed all, and reconstructed all, had come in final solution of the problem, to refer all to God, with a faith the most vital, and thereon to build up a theocratic society which has had no equal, and which, after more than five thousand years, still resists all innovation, all progress;-- proud of its institutions, of its beliefs, and of its immobility?

> **We shall see that Indian Society was the model of all ancient societies, who copied it more or less literally, or rather who preserved the traditions borne to the four quarters of the globe by successive emigrations.**

> The Priestly policy of investing themselves with the

prestige of divine authority, has, of course, had constant imitators and with the world's history before us, we may safely say that since then God has been but a docile instrument in the hands of the priest.

It was the inflexible law, that from no consideration what ever, by no brilliant action or service performed, could the individual obtain release from the caste in which he was born amelioration presenting itself to stimulate his energy, the Indian in mediaeval period after *Mahābhārata* war, whose every step, every act, from birth to death was checked, regulated by customs and laws, sunk into that life of dreams, of religious superstition, of fanaticism, and of materialism in which he still exists, and which still impels him to reject all change as an evil, all progress as a crime.

Unquestionably, the priests thus prepared for themselves a nation easy to govern, powerless to shake off the yoke, and even without energy to complain, they long enjoyed honours and devotion, riches and respects. But from the day when northern populations cast a jealous eye upon the reaches and splendour of Bharat, from the day when Mongol invasion led its flying hordes against them, in vain they tried to defend themselves, all their efforts were powerless to inspire for the struggle those people of whom they had made a herd of slaves, whom they had enervated to assure their domination. The Kṣatriays alone marched to death, but without power to retard the fatal hour of common wreck. And the Brahmins, while in their pagodas, imploring a God, powerless to save them, saw the prestige of their name and their political power crumble away, thanks to the very precautions they had adopted to preserve them.

India has since been the classic ground of invasions, and its people have submitted without murmur to each newly imposed yoke, perhaps even they may have gladly assisted the overthrow of those high castes which had so long ruled them.

We read in the preface to a Treatise on Legislation by Nārada, written by one of adepts, "Manu having written the laws of Brahmā in one hundred thousand *slokas* or distichs, which formed twenty four books and a thousand chapters, gave the work to Nārada, the sage of sages, who abridged it for the use of mankind, to twelve thousand verses, which he gave to a son of Bhṛgu named Sumati, who for the greater convenience of men reduced them to four thousand."

Manuṣyas (people inhabiting the equatorial regions) read only the abridgement of Sumati, while the Devas (people inhabiting the polar regions) study the primitive text.

"It is clear, "adds Sir William Jones, "that the laws of Manu, such as we possess them, and which comprise but 2,680 *slokas*, cannot be the work attributed to Sumati, which is probably that described under the name of Vṛddha-Mānava, -or ancient code of Manu, which has not yet been entirely reconstructed, although many passages of the book have been preserved by tradition, and are often cited by commentators. "*Mānava-Dharma Śāstra*" Manu divides persons into four personality types according to there professions.

1. *Brāhmaṇas* (visionary persons) involving themselves into the profession of research, teaching and learning. 2. *Kṣatriyas* (People endowed with fighting personality) involving themselves into the protection or defence activities). 3. *Vaiśyas* (people endowed with mercantile personality) involving themselves into marketing activities) and 4. *Śudras* (people endowed with labourer personality involving themselves into the production of various sorts in society).

According to Manu, a person of a peculiar personality type will prove more creative if he adheres to the occupation of his professional personality type. If a āperson of different professional personality type indulges into an occupation different from his personality type, he will not be able to deliver.

So *Mānava Dharma Śāstra* (Lib x, *ślokas* 91 etc.) further observes, if a person of professional personality of teaching and learning occupation indulges into the occupations of Merchants, or producers, they will also revert to the professional personality of merchants and producers.

A person of a professional personality of teaching and learning type should rather beg than reduce himself to the level of the artisans (producers), by the slightest handiwork."

The same work - (*śloka* 102, etc.) says "A person of teaching and learning personality type who has fallen into distress, should accept presents from any one; for, according to the law, it cannot happen to the perfectly pure, to be defiled."

"In teaching the Holy Scripture, in directing *yajñas*, in receiving presents in these forbidden cases, the persons of teaching and learning personality types commit no fault; if they are miserable they are as pure as water, or as fire."

"He, who finding himself in danger of death from starvation receives food from no matter whom, is no more soiled by pāpa, than is the subtle ether by mud."

"Ajigarta being famished, was on the point of destroying his son Śunaḥśepa; yet did he render himself guilty of no crime, for he sought relief from famine."

The commentator Kulluka Bhaṭṭa says that Ajigarta bound his son to a stake to sacrifice him as a burnt offering to the Lord, who, satisfied of his obedience, arrested his arm. This legend, finds its place in Biblical beginnings.

"Vāmadeva, who could perfectly distinguish between good and evil, did not become in the least impure, from having at a moment when presse7d by hunger, desired to eat the flesh of unclean animals."

"The rigid penitent Bharadvāja, alone with his son in a desert forest and tormented by hunger, accepted several cows from the humble artisan Vṛddha."

"Viśvāmitra, who was a holy person sinking from want resolved to eat the thigh of a dog, which he had received from a grave-digger."

It was the same for kings and all the other persons of different professional personality types; there was no crime equal to that attempting to change the situation, punished in this world by degradation and infamy, and in the other by the migration of souls, defiled by this transgression, into the bodies of the vilest animals.

From this moment of time, with the start of degradation in *Varṇa* system and origin of rigid caste system, the brilliant civilisation of India is arrested. Ignorance takes possession of the masses, who forgetful of their glorious past, dreaming only of sensual gratification, plunged into the most shameless corruption, encouraged by the then priests to maintain their own influence.

And priests reserved to themselves those ancient philosophic, moral and religious traditions, which became the privileged study of their caste, and a means of holding kings under their control by the double prestige of respect for religion and for learning.

For the simple and pure worship of primitive revelation and of the Vedas, they gradually substituted for the masses the adoration of numerous personages who, under the name of Devas, or angels and saints were regarded, some as immediate agents between God and his creatures, others as Brahmins, who, after having lived in the practice of every virtue on earth, had gone to be absorbed in the Divinity.

Brahmā, the pure Divine essence, had soon no more altars, and the prayers of mortals, to reach him, were to be addressed to those inferior beings whose images peopled pagodas and temples, and of which Buddha came later, to attempt the over throw, by a reform not without analogy to that attempted by Luther in after times.

This was the most terrible blow struck at ancient Indian Society, the finishing stroke to that work of decay and decrepitude whose effects we shall soon have occasion to study.

The priest shut himself up in dogma and mystery, professing himself the sole guardian, the only dispenser of truth in matters moral and religious, and calling to his aid the civil laws, which placed themselves servilely at his disposal, banished freedom of thought and reason, bent all will, all liberty under faith, and finally conceived the famous adages, which has since made its sufficiently successful way: "That there was nothing more agreeable to God than to believe without understanding; to bow down without knowledge; than to bring to the temple's porch an intelligence void of that which constitutes intelligence. - the rational belief of examination and comprehension."

We shall presently see Egypt, Judea, Greece, Rome, all antiquity, in fact, copy mediaeval Indian society in its castes, its theories, its religious opinions; and adopt its Brahmins, its priests, its levities as they had already adopted the language, legislation and philosophy in a corrupted form from the ancient Vedic Society whence their ancestors had departed through the world to disseminate the grand ideas of primitive revelation.

VI

Indian Origin
of
The Laws of Justinian
and
Civil death of the Code Napoleon

Observations of Louis Jacolliot, who was a Judge, are more interesting on the subject cited above. Those findings are placed hereunder:

> We have seen the Indian priests, after the fall (which was their work) of Vedic civilisation, institute for the security of their power, and with the design of imbuing their victims with salutary fear, this terrible penalty of rejection, partial or complete, from all caste, which placed the unhappy delinquent below the brute, since not the faintest social relation could be held with him without incurring degradation, and sinking to his level.

> Even the ties of family were broken; the children of the outcast became orphans, they were relegated to a tutor; his wife became a widow, and might re-marry if of a caste in which second marriage was not prohibited; his succession failed; and, finally, if he happened to be killed, the civil law touched not his murderer, who had simply to perform the religious ceremonies of purification, because he had been defiled by contact of a paria.

> From the soil of Mediaeval India, its birth-place, this institution of theocratic despotism quickly passed to the other countries that adopted it, in their turn, as an admirable instrument of domination; and thus did *the interdiction of water and of fire* come to be considered throughout antiquity a just and salutary penalty.

A modification it must be stated, was, however, introduced into the exercise of this severe repression.

Thus just as India, pronounced the sentence of expulsion from caste, for faults as well as for crimes; for religious as well as for social offences; similarly the different nations of antiquity tainted by Indian influence, also applied this penalty to political and religious crimes, treason, and conspiracies against all authority.

Crimes and offences against the person were subject to other laws.

This exception, however, did not include Egypt, which retained this practice in all its rigorous and arbitrary application, and it is easy to see the reason why.

After India, it is Egypt that exhibits to us the most painful example of stolid demoralisation and abasement of the people, who, deprived of all social and political role, deprived in some measure of the faculty of thinking, because deprived of the privilege of knowing, of acting, and of speaking; derived all initiative, their hours defined for refection, repose, and prayer, never long but docile instruments – producing machines to satisfy all the caprices of the small number of the elect, who elected themselves by aid of the religious idea, of terror and of lies.

Zoroaster, while retaining this penalty, ordained that it should only be applied to great offenders in the eyes of God and of men, and made it almost exceptional. In Greece (under the name of Ostracism, it was applied to men whose political influence was feared), interdiction of fire and water was scarce ever pronounced, except as *temporary,* and it does not appear that any special laws regulated its application.

Rome, after the example of India and of Egypt, ordained this mode of repression in its written law, under the name of *Capitis Minutio;* and, as the Oriental legislator Manu had admitted the partial or complete rejection of caste, so Roman legislation ordained degrees of this penalty: these were the great, the middle and the lesser *Minutio Capitis.*

By the first the citizen was deprived of all social and political rights; of all the rights of family; and placed in the same situation as the Egyptian and Indian – rejected from all caste.

Water and fire were prohibited in the same form, and as rigorously as Indian interdicted rice, water and fire.

He was not even allowed the resource of serving as a slave; and to kill him was not a crime.

By the second, all the rights of father and of master were suppressed; he had no longer any control over his children, who were emancipated by the fact, and his succession divided amongst his heirs.

By the third, or lesser *minutio capitis,* it but excluded the condemned from the magistracy, and from the service of the republic, leaving intact his paternal authority and the free disposition of his property.

Thus adopted into the written laws of Rome, this provision became, as we see, a penalty of common law.

These modes of penalisation personal degradation by withdrawing social and political rights, were of Eastern growth; and I am not in the least astonished to see the Osiris inventing such penalties under the influence of Indian penal code. The Rome was influenced by and followed the rule of the ancient world, I do not think a sufficient reason for denouncing her, but I feel a thrill of indignation when I see that our modern legislators had inscribed in our codes this rejection of caste, this *capitis minutio,* had prescribed, in fact, this civil death.

Civil death! Will it be believed that scarce fifteen years

ago, the victim of this penalty, had no longer on earth either wife, or children, or relations to articulate his name, to retain some little affection for one so unblest, and permit him, in default of hope, in the depths of his cell, to live a little upon memories?

And 1889 had passed over without daring to touch this hideous bequest of antiquity, preserved by that sacerdotal and fanatic middlc-agc, that sought to re-erect in Europe all the despotism and all the degenracies of Priestly class, by the division of castes, and domination of the priest.

Honour and remembrance, in the name of the people, in the name of humanity; honour and recollection in the history of painfully conquered progress, honour in the name of eternal justice, to the sovereign influence that in 1853 erased from our codes this odious relic of antique immortality and corruption!

We have said that in India, civil death, the complete exclusion from caste, was pronounced either by the judge for purely civil, or by the priest for religious offences. It was certainly necessary for Papal Rome, when in the middle ages attempting the role of Indian priests, to appropriate such customs; the instrument fitted her hand too well, and she would have invented, had she not inherited it from her illustrious ancestors.

Excommunication was nothing else than a weapon of despotism picked up in the temples, for the subjugation of people and of kings, and for triumph of the priest. We have seen it at work, in the middle ages, cursing people in their posterity – anathematising kings in their dynasty. We have seen Savonarola die at the stake for having exposed the disorders of Alexander VI., and the pious Robert, of France, abandoned by his friends and his most faithful servants, obliged to bend the knee under the hand of religious fanatic.

We have seen human hecatombs on the burning piles of

faith, and the alter reddened with blood.

Ages have passed away; we are but wakening to progress of free thought. But let us expect struggles without end, until the day when we shall have courage to arraign all sacerdotalism at the bar of liberty.

VII
Indian Origin
of
Egyptian Civilisation

Colonel Olcott says: "We have a right to more than suspect that India, eight thousand years ago, sent a colony of emigrants who carried their arts and high civilisation into what is now known to us as Egypt. This is what Brugsch Bey, the most trusted Egyptologer and antiquarian, says on the origin of the old Egyptians. Regarding these as a branch of the Caucasian family having a close affinity with the Indo-Germanic races, he insists that they 'migrated from India long before historic memory, and crossed that bridge of nations, the Isthmus of Suez, to find a new father-land on the banks of the Nile.' The Egyptians came, according to their own records, from a mysterious land (now shown to lie on the shore of the Indian ocean), the sacred Punt; the original home of their gods who followed thence after their people who had abandoned them to the valley of the Nile, led by Amon, Hor and Hathor. This region was the Egyptian 'Land of the Gods, ' Pa-Nater, in old Egyptian, or Holy land, and now proved beyond any doubt to have been quite a different place form the Holy land of Sinai. By the pictorial hieroglyphic inscription found (and intercepted) on the walls of the temple of the Queen Haslitop at Der-el-babri, we see that this Punt can be no other than India. For many ages the Egyptians traded with their old homes, and the reference here made by them to the names of the Princes of Punt and its fauna and flora, especially the nomenclature of various precious woods to be found but in India, leave us scarcely room for the smallest doubt that the old civilisation of Egypt is the direct outcome of that of the older India."

Mr. Pococke says: "At the mouths of the Indus dwell a seafaring people, active, ingenious, and enterprising as when, ages subsequent to this great movement, they themselves, with the warlike denizens of the Punjab, were driven from their native land to seek the far distant climes of Greece. The commercial people dwelling along the coast that stretches from the mouth of the Indus to the Coree, are embarking on that emigration whose magnificent results to civilisation, and whose gigantic monuments of art, fill the mind with mingled emotions of admiration and awe. These people coast along the shores of Mekran, traverse the mouth of the Persian Gulf, and again adhering to the sea-board of Oman, Hadramant, and Yeman (Eastern Arabia), they sail upto the Red Sea; and again ascending the mighty stream that fertilises a land of wonders, found the kingdoms of Egypt, Nubia, and Abyssinia. These are the same stock that, centuries subsequently to this colonisation, spread the blessings of civilisation over Hellas and her islands."

Mr. Pococke thus summarises his researches; "I would now briefly recapitulate the leading evidences of the colonisation of Africa from North-Western India and the Himalayan provinces. First, from the provinces or rivers deriving their names from the great rivers of India; secondly, from the towns and provinces of India or its northern frontiers; thirdly, from the Ruling Chiefs styled Ramas (Rameses), etc.; fourthly, similarity in the objects of sepulture; fifthly, architectural skill and its grand and gigantic character; and sixthly, the power of translating words, imagined to be Egyptian, through the medium of a modified Sanskrit."

Mr. Pococke then proceeds to subjoin "the opinions of

men of sound judgement in connection with Indian colonisation of Egypt."

The name "Nile" was given to the great river of Egypt by the Indian settlers there. "For about 10 miles below the Attock," says a critic, "the Indus has a clean, deep and rapid current, but for above a hundred miles further down to Kalabagh it become an enormous torrent. The water here has a dark lead colour and hence the name Nilab or Blue river given as well to the Indus as to a town on its banks, about 12 miles below Attock," As Aboasin (Abyssinia) in Africa, so here "we now observe the Nilab (the blue water) bestowing an appellation on the far-famed "Nile" of Egypt. **This is one of those facts which prove the colonisation of Egypt to have taken place from the coast of Sindh."**

Apart from historical evidence there are ethnological grounds to support the fact that the ancient Egyptians were originally an Indian people. Professor Heeren (Asiatic Nations) is astonished at the "physical similarity in colour and in the conformation of the head" of the ancient Egyptians and the Hindus. As regards the latter point, he adds: "As to the form of the head, I have now before me the skulls of a mummy and a native of Bengal from the collections of M. Blumenbach; and it is impossible to conceive anything more striking than the resemblance between the two, both as respects the general from and the structure of the firm portions. Indeed the learned Professor himself considers them to the most alike of any in his numerous collections."

After showing the still more striking similarity between the manners and customs, in fact, between the whole, social religious and political institutions of the two peoples, Professor Heeren (Historical Researches) says: "It is perfectly agreeable to Hindu manners the colonies from India, i.e. Banian families should have passed over into Africa, and carried with them their industry, and perhaps also their religious worship." He adds: "It is hardly possible to maintain the opposite side of questions viz., that the Indian were derived from the Egyptians, for it has been already ascertained that the country bordering on the Ganges was the cradle of Indian civilisation. Now, the Egyptians could not have established themselves in that neighbourhood, their probable settlement would rather have taken place on the Coast of Malabar."

Professor Heeren concludes : "Whatever weight may be attached to Indian tradition and the express testimony of Eusebius confirming the report of migrations from the banks of the Indus into Egypt, there is certainly nothing improbable in the event itself, as a desire of gain would have formed a sufficient inducement,"

After tracing the descent of Philippos of Macedon and his son, Alexander, from Bhili-Pos or Bhil-Prince and Hammon in Afghanistan, Mr. Pococke continues : "And these same Bhils, i.e., the Bhil Brahmans planted this same Oracle of Hammon in the deserts of Africa, whither I have already shown that they has sailed; where they founded Philai, i.e. Bhilai, the city of the Bhils, in lat. 24^0 North, long. 33^0 East.

Mr. Pococke, who made the subject his life-long study, says : "The early civilisation, then, the early arts, the indubitably early literature of India are equally the civilisation, the arts and literature of Egypt and of Greece – for geographical evidences, conjoined to historical fact and religious practices, now prove beyond all dispute that the two latter countries Egypt and Greece are the colonies of the India."

Louis   Jacolliot   Observes,   "Egypt,   from   its

geographical position, would necessarily be one of the first countries colonised (inhabited) by Indian emigrations, one of the first to receive the influence of that antique civilisation, which has radiated even to Europe."

She comments at length :

This truth becomes still more striking, when we study the institutions of this country, so constructed after those of Upper Asia, as to preclude other conclusion, and that the most obstinate prejudice must give way before the imposing mass of proofs that may be presented on the matter.

What I would charge myself especially to demonstrate is, the similitude of civil and political institutions of all the people of antiquity, the unity of idea in all; with India as initiatrix; as I shall, later, demonstrate the unity of all religious revelation, with India as the starting point.

What was the Government of Egypt, in looking back to its earliest time? Identically a copy of that of India, under the inspiration of the same legislator, or Manes, whose laws had been preserved by emigrant tradition, and served on the new soil to found a society similar to that of the mother country.

This name of Manu, or Manes, we have already said, is not a substantive, applying to an individual man; its Sanskrit signification is the man, par excellence, the legislator. It is a title aspired to by all the leaders of men of antiquity, which was decreed them in recompense of their services, or which they assumed to themselves as an honour.

Thus, as we have seen, the first Manu, of India, exercised on antique, the same influence as the Digest of Justinian on modern legislation.

Under the direction of this legislator, Egypt was naturally theocratic and sacerdotal; like India she had a worship and a hierarchy imposed upon her with the same severity, and with the same design of domination.

In the fist rank appeared the priest, protector and guardian of all civil and religious truth, controller of kings and people, emanation of God, anointed to the Lord, irresponsible in all his acts, in fact above all laws, as he was above all men.

After him comes the king, who is allowed to reign on condition that he but governs by the inspiration and the counsels of the priest.

Then lower, we find again, as in India, the trader obliged to aid the fortune of the two first *Varṇas* to pay for their luxury, their caprices, and their debaucheries; and lastly, the producer or artisan or worker, i.e. mechanics.

The priests reserved to themselves the exclusive knowledge of sciences. It was by physical phenomena which they alone understood, that they were able to work upon the spirits of kings and of crowds. They equally kept to themselves their sublime notions of God and the Trinity, the work of creation, and the immortality of the soul, leaving the mob to worship monsters, statues, images, and, as still and always in India, the ox, which we know was also a sacred animal in Egypt.

How must these priests of Thebes and Memphis, in the depths of their immense and sombre temples, which obliged to tear themselves from their high studies or their pleasures to promenade in pomp, and to the great joy of a semi-bovine people, that bull Apis, which they had created God in the pride of their power, and of their scorn of the servile nation they over rode!

And what amusement must they have derived from the

death of this bull, which they were obliged to replace, to maintain the dogma of his immortality!

How strictly did they for ages preserve the deposit of their knowledge, source of all their prestige! And by what terrible oaths must they have bound to themselves, those whom they consented to initiate!

As in Brahmanical society, the Egyptian priests decreed the impossibility of rising above that class in which each was born, thus stamping their institutions with the same seal of inertia and immobility.

The penal system was the same, and repression exercised by degradation, that is, by partial and complete caste-exclusion.

From which equally arose an outcast race of parias for our opinion, enforced by the logic of facts, is, that from this race or parias and of out-casts sprang the Hebrews, regenerated by Manes, Moses, or Moise.

The Egyptian priests, however, did not encounter a race of kings so pliant and so malleable as those of the Kṣatriyas, who never attempted to resist the authority of the Brahmins.

Whether that the vicars of Osiris at last became too exigent that the Pharaohs dreamt of an independence that flattered their ambition, that the hand of time desired to overthrow these senile institutions bequeathed by Post-Vedic Brahmanism, for the purpose of building up newer; after some ages of this sleep, from which India has not yet awakened. Egypt found herself disturbed by the strife of priests and kings, who, calling together their partisans, disputed, at the point of sword and lance, a power which was simply the appendage of the strongest, and for long years the people saw themselves governed alternately by dynasties of warriors, or of priests, as decided on the field of battle.

Hence, doubtless, the disappearance of ancient Egyptian civilisation from the world's stage. As in India, a theocratic government could only produce slaves, and so deeply rooted had become all the division of caste, that after the final triumph of kings they knew not how to break with the narrow traditions of the past, and regenerate their peoples, to lean upon them. They became, like Sesostris, wandering conquerors, carrying fire and sword into the territories of their neighbours, but incapable of founding anything; for the despotic power of an individual will always be powerless for the march of progress when each man of the nation is reduced to the state of a mere unit, instead of constituting an individuality.

You may build up blocks of stone, the astonishment of future ages, excavate lakes, turn the course of immense waters, construct gigantic palaces, train behind your triumphal car a hundred thousand slaves, the conquests of war servile history will weave you crowns; the Brahmins, the Levites, and the priests whom you will have gorged with honours and with riches, will chant your praises, present you to a prostrate people as an envoy of God, who accomplishes his mission; but for the thinker and the philosopher, for the history of humanity, and not that of dictators, you will have been but a mere stone of obstruction to that work of progress, by concord and by liberty, which is the end designed by God, and which each nation should strive to attain. You will have been but a brutal fact, come to show more clearly the weakness of human nature, and how the nations fall into decay.

Thus did ancient Egypt, after the fall of its theocratic government, sink, step by step, under the sway of priests and kings into ruin and oblivion; unprepared with a substitute, it has but to die.

So in collating these two antique countries, India and Egypt, do we see the same government, the same divisions of cast, the same institutions, produce the same results, and exclude these people from all part in the history of the future.

With such congruence before us, no one, I imagine, will appear to contest the purely Indian origin of Egypt unless to suggest that chance constructed in this country a civilisation modelled on that of the extreme East, or which would be still more absurd, that it was Egypt that colonised India, and Manu who copied Manes.

I can understand such an opinion being encouraged by people interested in denial, or ignorant of India. To them I shall merely reply: you have on your side but an affirmation and the stale objections which I have before heard, -- "And who tells you that it was not India that copied Egypt?" and you require that this affirmation shall be refuted by proofs leaving no room for even a shadow of doubt.

To be quite logical, then, deprive India of the Sanskrit, that language which formed all other; but show me in India a leaf of papyrus, a columnar inscription, a temple bas-relief tending to prove Egyptian birth.

Deprive India of all her remains of literature, legislation, and philosophy, which still there exist, preserved in the primitive language, and defying ages and profane hands – but show me what were the sources from which they were copied in Egypt.

Ignore, if you will, that great current of emigration from the Himalaya to Persia, Asia-Minor, and Arabia, of which science has recovered the traces. But show me colonising Egypt, sending out her sons over the globe. What language, what institutions, can we discover to-day, that she has bequeathed to the world?

Do we not see that the Egypt of Manes, sacerdotal Egypt had institution identical with those of India only in the first ages; that, forgetting, gradually, the tradition she had received, her kings shook off the yoke of priests, and that, from the time of Psameticus, she reversed the pure theocratic idea, to substitute for it the idea-Monarchical, which was thenceforth to govern the new civilisations? Do we not know that the divisions of caste were abolished under the Ptolemies?

Therein is the whole merit of Egypt, but it would be a mistake to assign to her others. She, first of antiquity, found energy to overthrow that government of the priest which had its birth in the extreme East, without, however, being able to escape the fall which its deleterious and corrupt influence had prepared for her.

Moreover, if we could allow ourselves to plunge into details; if we did not consider that those great similitude of principles, which are the base of the existence of nations, sufficiently support the thesis we maintain, we could prove, with the greatest facility, that the unity of God, admitted by the priests of Memphis, that Knef, Fta, and Fre, who are the three demiurgic gods, the three creators *par excellence,* the three persons of the Trinity in Egyptian theology, are symbolic Indian importation; that the belief in animals, the ibis and the bull, for instance, are superstitions brought from India by a radiation of which it is it easy to follow the march; that matter, as the primitive atom, called Bouto by the initiated, and represented under the fecund form of an egg, is but a souvenir of the Vedas and of Manu, who compares the germ of all things to "an egg, brilliant as gold."

Let is suffice to have indicated these great points of contact which, to us, explain ancient Egypt, by India and Brahminical influences, and logically raise, as far as possible, a corner of the veil that obscures and envelopes the cradle of all peoples.

VIII
Indian Origin
of
Greek-Civilisation

The Indian emigrations to Greece is the subject of such fascinating interest that eminent scholars and archaeologists have devoted their time and learning to unravel the mystery connected with the origin of the race, whose splendid achievements in peace and war yet stand unrivalled in Europe. Colonel Tod and Colonel Wilford laid the foundations of system of enquiry in this branch of historical research, on which Mr. Pococke has raised the marvellous structure of "India in Greece," which is now available in a revised and re-edited form as 'Indian origin of Greece and Ancient World' which stands firm and solid, defying the violence and fury of the windy criticism of ignorant critics and the hail and sleet of certain writers on Indian Archaeology, blinded by inveterate prejudices. Mr. Pococke quotes chapter and verse in proof of his assertions, and proves beyond all shadow of doubt the Indian origin of the ancient Greeks.

After describing the Grecian society during the Homeric times, Mr. Pococke says: "The whole of this sate of society, civil and military, must strike everyone as being eminently Asiatic, much of it specifically Indian. Such it undoubtedly is. And I shall demonstrate that these evidences were but the attendant tokens of an Indian colonisation with its corresponding religion and language. I shall exhibit dynasties disappearing from Western India to appear again in Greece: clans, whose martial fame is still recorded in the faithful chronicles of North-western

India, as the gallant bands who fought upon the plains of Troy."

"But, if the evidences of Saxon colonisation in this island (Great Britain) – I speak independently of Anglo-Saxon history – are strong both from language and political institutions, the evidences are still more decisive in the parallel case of an Indian colonisation of Greece-not only her language, but her philosophy, her religion, her rivers, her mountains and her tribes; her subtle turn of intellect, her political institutes, and above all the mysteries of that noble land, irresistibly prove her colonisation from India. **"The primitive history of Greece," adds the author, "is the primitive history of India."**

There are critics who concede the derivation of Greek from the Sanskrit, but stop short of the necessary inference that the people who spoke the farmer language were the descendants of those who spoke the latter. Of such, Mr. Pococke asks : "Is it not astonishing that reason should so halt half-way in its deduction as to allow the derivation of the Greek from an Indian language, and yet deny the personality of those who spoke it; or, in other words, deny the settlement of an Indian race in Greece?"

The word Greek itself signifies the Indian origin of the ancient Greeks. The royal city of Magedhanians or Kings of Magadha was called "Raja Griha." "The people or clans of Griha were, according to the regular patronymic form of their language, styled Graihka, whence the ordinary derivative Graihakos (Graikos) Graceus or Greek. This shows that the Greeks were migrators from Magadha; which fact is still further strengthened when we consider that their predecessors in their adopted country were also inhabitants of Magadha. These people were Pelasgi. They were so-called because they emigrated from Pelasa, the ancient name for the province of Bihar, in Āryāvartta. Pelasgo is a derivative form of Pelasa, whence the Greek Pelasgo. The theory is further strengthened when we find that Asius, one of the early poets of Greece, makes King Pilasgus spring from "Gaia". This "Gaia" is no other than the "Gaya" the capital city of Pelaska or Bihar.

Aeubaea was colonised by "Eu-babooyas," the Bahoojas or warrior par excellence. The Makedonians (Macedon=Magada) were the inhabitants of Magadha, the same province. The people of Bihar or Maghada, it appears migrated in several tribal groups to Greece; and their migrations are marked by the different names they gave to the part or parts of their adopted country. Says Mr. Pococke: "The Buddhas have brought with them into Thessaly the far-famed mythological but equally historical name of 'Cilas,' the fabulous residence of Cuvera (Kuber), the (Indian) god of wealth, and the favourite hunt of Śiva, placed by the Indian among the Himalayan mountains, and applied to one of the loftiest peaks lying to the north of the Mānasa lake.

Many other tribes of the Kṣtriyas migrated to Greece and the isles of the Archipelago. The Boeotians were the "Baihootian," Rajput dwellers on the banks of Behoot (Jehlum): the Cossopaei were the Kashmirians so-called from Kaśyapa, the founder of Kashmir. The Hellopes were the Chiefs of the Hela tribe and their country "Hellados, Hella-desa." The names, Mount Kerketius (Kertecha range in Afghanistan), Locman (Lughman of Afghanistan), and Mount Titarus (the Tatara Pass of Afghanistan), Mount Othrys (Sanskrit name *adri* for mountain), Matan Astæ (Matan-Vasti "the dwelling place of the Matan, a tribe of Kashmir), Kestrine (Kṣatriya, warrior caste, and *ina*, chief), all point to the fact that many of the migrators were originally inhabitants of the North-western parts of India.

Speaking of the Hindus having reared a Mythological superstructure on physical facts in making Mount Kailāśa, the abode of the gods, Mr. Pococke says: "Thus it was with the native of Indus and of the rocky heights of Hela, when he became a settler in the Hellas; and thus it was with his polished descendent in Athens, who though called a Greek was yet as thoroughly Sindian in his tastes, religion, and literature as any of his forefathers."

"The land of Hellas, a name so dear to civilisation and the arts," says Pococke, "was so-called from the magnificent range of heights situated in Bilochistan, styled the 'Hela' mountains..... The chiefs of this country were called Helaines or the chiefs of the Hella. The formation of the term Helenes in Sanskrit would be identical with the Greek. Hel-en (the Sun-king) is said to have left his kingdom to Aiolus, his eldest son, while he sent for Dorus and Zuthus to make conquests in foreign lands. Haya is the title of a renowned tribe of Rajput warriors. They were called Asii or Aśva, and their chiefs, 'Aśva-pas,' and to use the words of Conon, as quoted by Bishop Thirlwall, "the patrimony of Aiolus (the Haiyulas) is described as bounded by the river Asopus (Aśva-pas) and the Enipeus," Such, then, was the Asopus, the settlement of the Haya tribes, the Aśva chiefs, the sun worshippers, the children of the Sun-king or Helen, whose land was called in Greek Hellados, in Sanskrit, Hela-des (Hela, Heia; *des*, iand). Of Achilles, sprung from a splendid Rajput stock.

The Linguistic proofs cited at page 21 above are the most irrefutable proof of the influence of India on Greece. In fact, from the Sanskrit was formed the language of Greece.

Louis Jacolliot further elaborates this subject as under:

In fact all the names of fabulous and heroic epochs of gods and demi-gods, all the names of people that Greece has transmitted to us, are nearly pure Sanskrit. We may say, too, that the greater part of the words which compose Greek language and its syntax, have the Sanskrit origin; and, if discussion should be raised on this ground, it would be easy for us to show that this assertion is simply a mathematical truth, which, as such, may boldly affirm and prove itself. We shall, therefore, devote but a few lines to the Cretan legislator, whose written work, indeed, has not reached us.

Minos is incontestably of Asiatic origin; Greek history makes him come from the India into Crete, where the people, struck with his wisdom, besought his legislation. He then travelled into Egypt, of which he studied the institutions; Asia, Persia, and the banks of the Indus, saw him in turn interrogate their traditions and antique legislation; then he returns to give to the Cretans his book of the law, which was soon after, adopted by all Greece.

It was probable after, and as a consequence of, these travels, that he received the name of Minos, of which, as we have already said, the Sanskrit root signifies *legislator;* and we conceive, that in consideration of his travels in Egypt and in Asia, and of his Oriental origin, we are safe in our association of him with Manu, and with Manes, and in expressing the opinion attested by facts, since the sought instruction at primitive source; that he derived his inspiration from the works of Indian and Egyptian legislators; and that he held it imperative to assume the honorary title which the gratitude of peoples had decreed to his two precursors.

We cannot too often repeat that these words, Manu,

Manes, Minos, and Moses, are not proper names, but significant titles born by antique legislators, just as the kings of India bore the title of Kṣatriays, of Persia that of Xerxes, and those of Egypt that of Pharaoh.

Contenting ourselves, then, with the proofs already given in the first chapter of this work, we shall not inquire whether the Greek feasts, Pythonesses and mysteries of Brahmanism. Moreover, Greece, that was so largely influenced by Indian literature, language, and philosophy, quickly ignoring its fabulous origin, soon learned to laugh at its Olympus – the debauched gods of a superstitious tradition – and, as we have seen, to advance with a firm step in the way opened to it by the *Śāstras*, to the conquest of untrammelled thought.

Had not Rome appeared, with her brutal invasion, to dry up the energy and the life of this admirable country, long since had all those problems of progress and liberty which have not yet ceased to agitate Europe with revolutions, been solved by the sons of Hellas, by those descendants of free and primitive Indian society.

Although the family of the Eumolpides, priests of Ceres, who were apparently a caste of Levites, had also enjoyed great influence in Greece at an early period, it does not appear that they ever succeeded in confiscating the their own profit, the government of the nation; and to that fact, chiefly, must be attributed the considerable development of human thought on this narrow soil, which had succeeded in establishing, at home, the reign of democracy and of liberty, at an epoch when all political and religious despotism joined hands to enslave the world.

We know, in fact, that from the fall of Hippias, until the time of the Macedonian and Roman conquests, Athens affords modern nations the example of a popular government, in which liberty had brought to perfection all the glories of literature, of philosophy, and of arts.

The citizen, by universal suffrage, elected his archons, his magistrates, his functionaries; the right of peace and of war, the legislative power, the discussion of all the great interests of the republic belonged to the general assembly of the people, to which every free man brought the aid of his word and his vote, under penalty of forfeiture of his rights.

It was the first appearance in the world of the national idea, substituted for that servile obedience to the caprices of a master, which had until then governed societies.

India (of post *Mahābhārata* period) groans and dies under the priest, Egypt, inheritor of this tradition, ends by overthrow of theocracy, to cast itself into the arms of kings, and Greece, remembering the East, and the sacerdotal domination which she had rejected, to expand herself on a freer soil, makes another stride of progress, and, replacing the slave by the citizen, institutes the government of the nation by the nation.

Hence was born the modern spirit.

Thus these first Indian emigrations by the South, after long subjection to revelation and the priest, had, step by step, effected their overthrow, and a commencement of progress by independence and by reason.

Why was it that the second steam of emigration by the Himalayas and the plains of the North, which brought into Europe the Scandinavian, Germanic and Slave tribes (no doubt retarded by the aridity of soil and the rigors of a new climate), could not so rapidly attain civilisation as the nations of the South, and swooped upon them, one fine morning, to destroy them?

Wild children of the forests, worshippers of Odin and of Skanda, these people had retained the legendary souvenir of their origin; their songs and their poems, full of Oriental traditions, spoke to them of restoration to their cradle lands and cloudless skies, and, in their search of Asgard, the city of the sun, they encountered Rome, and the ancient world disappeared.

And the new world slept for more than fifteen centuries under a domination not less sacerdotal, not less tyrannic, than that of antiquity, before recovering the grand souvenirs, the grand social and political truths bequeathed it by Greece.

IX
Indian Origin
of
Persian Civilisation

Mr. Pococke says: "I have glanced at the Indian settlements in Egypt, which will again be noticed, and I will now resume my observation from the lofty frontier, which is the true boundary of the European and Indian races. The Parasoos, the people of Parasu Ram, those warriors of the Axe, have penetrated into and given a name to Persia; they are the people of Bharata; and to the principal stream that pours its waters into the Persian Gulf they have given the name of Eu-Bharat-es (Euphrates), the Bharat Chief."

Professor Max Müller's testimony (*Science of Language*, p. 242) is decisive on the point discussing the word 'Arya,' he says, "But it was more faithfully preserved by the Zoroastrians, who migrated from India to the North-west and whose religion has been preserved to us in the Zend Avesta, though in fragments only." He again says: "The Zoroastrians wore a colony from Northern India."

Professor Heeren says, "In point of fact the Zend is derived from the Sanskrit, and a passage in Manu (chapter 10, *ślokas* 43-45) makes the Persians to have descended from the Indian Kṣatriyas.

Pococke says, "The Old name of the country, Iran, was given by the first settlers there, who were Airan, the descendants of Aira, the son of Pururavas, the son of Buddha of the Lunar race. (Airan is plural of Aira). These settlers had been expelled from India after long wars spoken of by ancient chronicles of Persia as wars between Iran and Turan. Turan being a corrupt form of Suran, Sura the Sun, the sun tribes. The tribe of "Cossoei" seen near the banks of the Tigris, are the people of Kāśī, the classical name of Benaras."

Sir W. Jones (Sir William Jones Works, vol.1,pp 82-83) says: "I was not a little surprised to find that out of ten words in Du Perron's Zend Dictionary, six or seven were pure Sanskrit.

Mr. Haug, in an interesting essay on the origin of Zoroastrian religion, compares it with Vedic, and points out the originally-close connection between the Vedic and the Zoroastrian religions, customs and observances. After comparing the names of divine beings, names and legends of heroes, sacrificial rites, religious observances, domestic rites, and cosmographical opinions that occur both in the Vedic and Avesta writings, he says: "In the Vedas as well as in the older portions of the Zend-Avesta (see the Gathas), there are sufficient traces to be discovered that the Zoroastrian relation arose out of a vital struggle against a form which the Vedic religion has assumed at a certain early period. After contrasting the names of the Indian Gods and the Zoroastrian deities, Professor Haug says: "These facts throw some light upon the age in which that great religious struggle took place, the consequence of which was the entire separation of the Ancient Iranians from the Brahmans and the foundation of the Zoroastrian religion.

According to Harbilas Sarda, "It is not an easy matter

to ascertain the exact period at which the Indian
colonisation of Persia took place. It is certain, however,
that it took place long before the Mahābhārata." Colonel
Tod Says: "Ajameda, by his wife, Nila, had five sons,
who spread their branches on both sides of the Indus.
Regarding three the Purāṇas are silent, which implies
their migration to distant regions. Is it possible they
might be the origin of the Medes? These Medes are
descendants of Yayāti, third son of the patriarch, Manu:
and Madai, founder of the Medes, was of Japhet's line.
Aja Meda, the patronymic of the branch of Bajaswa, is
from Aja's goat.' The Assyrian Mede in Scripture is
typified by the goat.

Here Harbilas Sarda's arguments are worth noticing .
He says, "Apart from the passage in Manu, describing the
origin of the ancient Persians, there is another argument
to support it. Zoroaster, the Prophet of the Ancient
Persians, was born after the emigrants from India had
settled in Persia, long enough to have become a separate
nation. Vyāsa held a grand religious discussion with
Zoroaster at Balkh in Turkistan, and was therefore his
contemporary. Zanthus of Lydia (470 BCE), the earliest
Greek writer, who mentions Zoroaster, says that he lived
about six hundred years before the Trojan War (which
took place about 1800 BCE). Aristotle and Endoxus place
his era as much as six thousand years before Plato, others
five thousand years before the Trojan War (See Pliny :
Historia Naturialis, XXX, 1-3). Berosos, the Babylonian
historian makes him a king of the Babylonians and the
founder of a dynasty which reigned over Babylon
between BCE 2200 and BCE 2000. It is, however, clear
that the Indian colonisation of Persia took place anterior
to the Great War of *Mahābhārata*."

In the first chapter (Fargard) of the part which bears

the name Vendidad of their sacred book (which is also
their most ancient book), Hurmuzd or God tells Zapetman
(Zoroaster): "I have given to man an excellent and fertile
country. Nobody is able to give such a one. This land lies
to the east (of Persia), where the stars rise every
evening." "When Jamshed (The leader of the emigrating
nation), came from the highland in the east to the plain,
there were neither domestic animals nor wild, nor men."
According to Count Bjornstjerna, "The country alluded to
above from which the Persians are said to have come can
be no other than the North-west part of ancient
India–Afghanistan and Kashmir being to the east of
Persia, as well as highland compared to the Persian
plains."

Mr. Pococke says, "The ancient map of Persia,
Colchis, and Armeni is absolutely full of the most distinct
and startling evidences of Indian colonisation, and, what
is more astonishing, practically evinces, in the most
powerful manner, the truth of several main points in the
two great Indian poems, the Rāmāyaṇa and the
Mahābhārata. The whole map is positively nothing less
than a journal of emigration on the most gigantic scale."

Here the findings of Louis Jacolliot are also
noteworthy. Accordingly :

> The name of the reformer, who came to play in Persia,
> the part of Celestial Messenger, is, in Persian, Zerdust;
> in Zend, Zertochtro; in Pehlvi, Zoradot. There different
> expressions are but variations of the primitive name,
> which is, in Sanskrit, *Sūryastara* (who restores the
> worship of the sun), from which comes this name of
> Zoroaster, which is itself but a title as signed to a
> political and religious legislator.
>
> **As his Sanskrit origin sufficiently indicates,
> according even to the testimony of history,**

Zoroaster was born in Upper Asia, that is, in India. After having passed to greater part of his life in study of the religion and the laws of India, his travels led him into Persia, where, encountering the most superstitious practices, he undertook to reform them, and to endow that country with a religion more comformable to morals and to reason.

Zoroaster was, without doubt, a fugitive from the pagodas and temples of India, who, wishing the people to profit by the truths and sublime knowledge which the priests reserved exclusively to themselves, but fearing their power if he preached in India, sought a country less immediately under their control.

Arrived at the court of the kings Gouchtasp and Isfendiar, he opened their eyes to means of withdrawing themselves from the influence of Brahmins, from whom they held their investiture; and, thanks to this clever temptation, having gained them to his cause, he was permitted to preach the new doctrine, and to submit to his laws the entire of Iran, even to the Sind (Indus); that is, to the very frontier sanctuary of Brahmanical power.

So, Luther, afterwards, by showing the German princes the possibility of shaking off the despotic and capricious yoke of the popes, enrolled them in the camp of reform.

Only, the great monk of Wittemberg, instead of striking the imagination of the peoples, like his predecessors, by prodigies and wonders, instead of presenting himself as a celestial envoy, trusted the success of his mission to appeal in the name of reason. Doubtless, had he lived some years earlier, he would have been obliged to surround himself with a halo of mystery, to impress the crowd – only raising the veil to the initiated few.

So certain is the Indian origin of Zoroaster, that history itself informs us that the Brahmins, furious at the desertion of this false brother, who had aimed the first blow at their power, summoned him to appear before them to explain his schism; and that, failing to entice him into the trap, they marched at the head of a powerful army, from Eastern to the re-conquest of Western India (Iran), which had withdrawn itself from their dominion. Defeated by Zoroaster, they were constrained to retire, and leave him to pursue the new work in peace.

In his teaching, Zoroaster innovated little upon the priestly system. He divided the people into castes, at the head of which, and above kings, he placed the Magi, or priests, regulated public and private life, and, finally, adopted a penal system similar to that which we have seen establish itself in India and in Egypt. His religious reform was only such in this sense, that rejecting the many superstitions into which Indian priests had allowed the multitude to sink, he instructed all in the religious principles of the Vedas, that is, the unity of God in the Trinity.

He gave to the Divine essence, *par excellence*, to the creative power, the name of Zervane-Akerene.

To the presiding principle of preservation, he gave the name of Ormuz. To that of decomposition and reconstruction, the name of Ahriman.

It is exactly the Indian *Trimūrti* (Trinity), with their symbolic attributes and role in creation.

Zoroaster did not extirpate all the superstition's which he, perhaps, intended to overthrow; freethinker at first, he soon found himself in advance of his age, and that the populations were not ripe for such institutions as he had conceived. Each reformer, also, has always, unhappily, a train of disciples behind him, whose personal ambitions intervene to retard advance, and modify primitive principles.

The Magi soon became an initiated class – a monopolising class, like all sacerdotal castes. Class-divisions assisted them plausibly to bend the people to their authority, and, as in India, as in Egypt, mysteries, sacrifices, processions were needed for the people who would no more than those others, have comprehended a worship from all pomp and charlatanism. Hence those monstrous hecatombs, those gigantic festivals of the Sun or of fire, of which antiquity so long retained the recollection.

The disciples of Zoroaster, in their profusion of legends of the Master, relate that one day, as he prayed in a high mountain in the midst of thunders and lightning that divided the heavens in all parts, he was taken up into heaven, and saw Ormuz, face to face in all the êclat of his grandeur and his majesty, and received from him the divine instructions which 'he was, later, to reveal to man.

When Zoroaster returned to earth he brought with him the book of the law, called Nosks, which he had written under the direction of the Supreme Being.

This book is nothing else than a recollection of the Vedas and of the sacred book of the Indians, which, in his youth, Zoroaster had studied in India.

Thus the influence of India on Persia and in all the countries of Sind, has all the authentication of historic truth, Here tradition, less obscure than the Egypt to all the proofs drawn from similarity of religious and political institutions, adds the testimony of history of those far back times in which we may follow the traces of Zoroaster from India of the East, to India of the West, from the banks of the Ganges to the banks of the Indus.

Do we now understand how all these Indian traditions, escaping from the great focus by Arabia and Egypt, Persia and Asia-Minor, were able, with modifications, to reach Judea, Greece, and Rome?

In concluding this, let us remark that Zoroaster, like, Manu and Manes, assigned himself midst the people he came to rule or regenerate, a celestial origin and a celestial mission.

X
Indian Origin
of
Roman Civilisation

Rome, Italy or Etruria are synonym to each other. From 7th century B.C. to 2nd century B.C. a very large part of Italy was also known as Etruria. According to Pococke, Romans were the descendants of colonists from Bharat. The Romans were the inhabitants of the Trojans, inhabitants of that part of Asia Minor in which Hindu settlements had long been established. In fact, the warriors of Abanti race who participated in the famous Trojan War were the descendants of Avanti race of Malwa of Bharat. This fact was also corroborated by Pococke. Thus it is clear from the above fact that the Rome was inhabited by the stream of Kṣatriyas of Avati race of Malwa.

Niebuhr says, 'Rome is not a Latin name.' Mr. Pococke says it is 'Rama'. The Sanskrit long 'ā' is replaced by 'o' or 'w' of the Greeks, as 'Poseidon' and 'Poseidan'. The fact is that Rama has been regarded as an ideal monarch in Rome as elsewhere in the world. That is why from modern Siam to the Hunza kingdom and Pharaohs of ancient Egypt, every monarch proudly used to style himself as Rama 1 or Ramesis 1 or Ramesis II, etc. The Rome is named after the name of Rama of Rāmāyaṇa is proved by the existence of scores of paintings of Ramayanic episodes in ancient Italian Homes. P.N. Oak has given some remarkable paintings/pictures depicting the episodes of Rāmāyaṇa in the ancient homes in Italy discovered in archaeological excavations. Some of the pictures are reproduced below.

The Roman Republican coins depicting Ramayanic seen of Rama, Sita and Lakshman walking in the Jungle.

A painting in Etruscan Museum in Vatican in Rome (Italy) depicts a Ramayanic seen of Vānara-rāja, literally meaning Monkey Chief Vali abducting Tara, the wife of his brother Sugreev.

Below are given some other pictures depicting various Ramayanic seens found painted in the Etruscan Museum in the Vatican in Rome and ancient homes in Italy.

The above picture Etruscan Museum depicts Ramayanic seen of Lava and Kush capturing a sacrificial horse led by their father and driving it away to sage Valmiki's hermitage.

Yet another proof of Rāma origin of Rome is that another Italian city, situated on the Adriatic coast, diagonally opposite to Rome, is named Ravenna, after Ravana, the adversary of Rāma. Upon this Pococke reacts, 'Behold the memory of Ravana still preserved in the city of Ravenna, and see on the western coast, its great rival Rāma or Roma.' This Rome-Revenna pair of cities proves without any shadow of doubt that Rome was founded by the Bhāratīya Kṣatriyas of Sūrya Vañśa (solar dynasty) after the name of Rāma.

Having their Bhāratīya origin, the Roman people had many cultural traditions common to Hindus. Fanny Parks describes the similarity of funeral rites between Hindus and Romans. According to her, 'The nearest relation closed the eyes and mouth of the deceased..... The corpse was then laid on the ground, bathed and anointed with perfumes. The body, dressed in the best attire which the deceased had worn when alive, was laid on a couch in the vestibule, with the feet onwards; the couch was sometimes decked with leaves and flowers. Romans....early adopted the custom of burning (cremandi vel comburendi) from the Greeks....but was afterwards gradually dropped upon the introduction of Christianity. It had fallen into disuse about the end of 4rth century.' Fanny Parks observes, 'The Romans worshipped their founder Romulus as a God, under the name Quirinus...' The fact is that their Lord called himself Romulus after the ideal of Lord Rama of Ramāyaṇa. P.N. Oak is absolutely right when he says 'the name Quirinus is a Greeco-Roman corruption of the word 'Krishna' of Mahābhārata'.

Franz Cumont observes, 'Roman soldiers learned to revere 'Ma' the great goddess....the rites of her cult were even more sanguinary.... clad in black robes..' The goddess 'Ma' in black robes was nothing else than 'Kāli Mā' of Bharat.

Thus Rome, that is called the eternal city, was founded in 753 BC, by an Avanti solar dynasty king from Malwa, Bharat who titled himself as Romulus after Rama on the banks of Tiber river and seven hills - Palatine, Capitolin, Quirinal, Viminal, Isquilin, calian and Abentine - surround it. In the beginning, it was ruled by Etruscan family. Etruscans were also colonists from Bharat who penetrated into Italy sometime before or about the colonisation of Greek. Of the Asiatic tribe called 'Asor', Count Bjornstjerna says, 'It seems to be the same tribe which came by sea to Etruria.' This is the reason why the Etruscans had a system of religion in many respects similar to that of the Hindus.

Culture and Religion in Ancient Rome

Evidences in Rome suggests that Bhāratīyas migrated to Rome twice. The first emigrants developed there an Etruscan culture. Etruscans followed Vedic culture. They named Rome after Rama and devoutly caricatured Ramayanic events on the walls of their homes. Such drawings are now on display in various museums in Italy. They used to worship all the Vedic deities. At numerous places in Italy, the idols of Shiva, Ganesh and other Vedic deities have been found abundantly. Famous historian P. N. Oak has given some pictures of Shiva and Ganesh which tells about the Vedic religion of ancient Etruscans or ancient Romans (see page 115).

The ancient Romans were the worshipper of 'Kali Mā'. They had the funeral system of dead similar to that of Bharat. It is noteworthy here that ancient Romans used to wear Bhāratīya style dhoti and apply tilak (Sandal paste mark on their foreheads) like Bhāratīyas. On the next page are given pictures of ancient Italy's Eutruscan emperor and Pompey (Consul of Rome) both have been shown applying tilak or Sandalwood mark on their forehead. These pictures appears on page 300 and 237 respectively in the book titled *History of Rome* by Smith quoted by P.N. Oak at age 812 and 813.

Pompey, the consul of Rome, applying a Tilak (Sandalwood mark)

Lucius Cornelius Sulla Roman general or statesman who held the office of the consul twice wearing Tilak mark (Sandalwood mark) on his head.

During the second post-Mahābhārata immigration of Bhāratīyas to Rome, Vedic Dharma started disintegrating into various religions in and outside Bharat. Instead of following the notions of Vedic Dharma, people tended towards religion, which is different from Dharma. The religion of Indian settlers of Rome was up to some extent similar to that of their contemporary Indian settlers of Greece.

Here, one more prominent thing is that Dhoti was the earliest dress of both Roman men and women. It was worn from the time of Etruscan kings through the 4th century AD. We may depict here some more pictures of Etruscan kings in Dhoti.

Ancient Italy's Etruscan Emperor Nerva wearing Indian dhoti

Augustus emperor from 27 BC to 14 AD

Lord Shiva standing over a public fountain called 'Fountain of Naptune' (Fontana di Nettuno) at Eponymous square, Plazza Nettuno next to Plazza Maggiore in Bologna, Italy. Notice the trident of Shiva.

Roman gods were having more characteristics of Bhāratīya Devas whereas Greek gods were having characteristic like that of Asuras indulging in mutual jealousy, envy and ever fighting for the possession of women.

Jacolliot observes on Indian Origin of Roman civilisation like this :

It might be said that we here offer proofs borrowed precisely from those fabulous and heroic epochs which we profess to explode; the answer is easy. Maintaining that these fabulous and heroic times are but Indian and Asiatic traditions, admitting them as the souvenir of a common origin, it becomes, we conceive, a *bonne fortune* for our theory, to find, at every corner of the colonised earth, the legend that makes the colonist come from India. And if of this legend are begotten customs and institutions, still better establishing that affinity and that origin, have we not a right to maintain that we have established the matter as completely as possible?

We have seen that Rome was indebted to India for her grand principles of legislation. If the Latin, as well as the Greek, is also, as modern science admits, derived from the Sanskrit; if, as is incontestable, the Roman Olympus is but an emanation of the Greek Olympus, which itself had its birth in the mysteries of India, of Persia, and of Egypt, what more shall we say to render the truth more true?

Had not Rome her castes, like the more ancient nations, her predecessors? And if those divisions were less important, and more easily subverted, ought we not to attribute that result to the infiltration of younger blood on a richer soil, producing the necessaries of life, doubtless, with less facility; but, for that reasons, requiring more labour and more energy?

Does not this constitution of the Roman people, as priests, senators, patricians, and plebeians, represent a feebler image of Indian society? Was not the impossibility of rising from an inferior to a superior class, equally decreed? Do we not perceive, in fact, at the very beginning of this new civilisation, the same programme of domination by the systematic subjugation and degradation of the masses?

And if we ask whence Rome could have acquire the idea of these institutions, we find that she sent her sages and her legislators into Greece, Egypt, and, no doubt, even to Asia, to explore the great focus of the enlightenment which from India had radiated over the entire ancient world.

At this time the senile traditions of Brahmanism were every where in decay. Buddha, it is true, had been expelled from India. Zoroaster was revolutionising

Western India and Persia. To the Sacerdotal era in Egypt had succeeded the Monarchic period, and Greece, repudiating her cloudy past, was preparing her Republican institutions. Obviously, the attempt made at Rome to regenerate this state of things, by the power of priests and of certain privileged classes, could but result in a succession of struggles and civil wars, to end, soon or late, in a social and political equality, which the people had already began to dream of and to desire.

In vain did the higher classes, to preserve their power, dazzle the eyes and employ the energy of the populations with wars and conquests; they were obliged to give way, and gradually bow to the freshening breeze that threatened to destroy them.

But, if social divisions were abolished, or their influence paralysed, not less did the ineffaceable signs of primitive Oriental tradition remain in customs and laws which retain even amongst modern nations the stamp of their origin.

We shall not protract these reflections. Moreover, does not Latin loudly proclaim its Sanskrit parentage? And have we not already, in our preceding chapters on legislation, demonstrated the direct and preponderating influence of India on Rome?

XI

Indian Origin
of
Ethiopian Civilisation

According to Count Bjornstjerna, "The ancient geographers called by name Ethiopia all that part of Africa which now constitutes, Nubia, Abyssinia, Sanaor, Darfur and Dongola was first inhabited by the Indians. Sir W. Jones (vol.1, p. 426) says, "Ethiopia and Hindustan were possessed or colonised by the same extraordinary race (Hindus)"

Philostratus (quoted by Pococke) introduces the Brahman Iarchus by stating to his auditor that the Ethiopian were originally an Indian race compelled to leave India for impurity contracted by slaying a certain monarch to whom they owed allegiance."

Eusebius states that the Ethiopians emigrating from the River Indus settled in the vicinity of Egypt.

In Philostratus, an Egyptian is made to remark that he had heard from his father that the Indians were the wisest of men, and that the Ethiopians, a colony of the Indians, preserved the wisdom and usage of their forefathers and acknowledged their ancient origin. We find the same assertion made at a later period, in the third century, by Julius Africanus, from whom it has been preserved by Eusebius and Syncellus."

Cuvier quoting Syncellus, even assigns the reign of Amenophis as the epoch of the colonisation of Ethiopia from India.

The ancient Abyssinians (Abusinians), as already remarked, were originally migrators to Africa from the banks of Abuisin, a classical name for the Indus.

As will appear from the accounts of the commercial position of India in the ancient world, commerce on an extensive scale existed between ancient India and Abyssinia, and we find Indians in large numbers settled in the latter country, "whence also," says Colonel Tod, (vol.II, p.309, footnote) "The Hindu names of towns at the estuaries of the Gambia and Senegal rivers, the Tamba cunda and another Cundas." he continues : "A writer in the Asiatic Journal (vol. IV, p. 325) gives a curious list of the names of places in the interior of Africa, mentioned in Park's Second Journey which are shown to be all Sanskrit and most of them actually current in India at the present day."

XII

Indian Origin
of
Civilisation in Asia Minor

The Chaldeans were originally migrators from India. Chaldea is a corruption of cul (kula) (family or tribe) and deva (a god). The country, colonised by the tribe of Devas, was called Kuldeo or Chaldea, whence the word Chaldeans. Cunt Bjornstjerna says, "The Chaldeans, the Babylonians and the inhabitants of Colchis derived their civilisation from India.

Mr. Pococke says: "The tribe 'Abanti' who fought most valiantly in the Trojan War were no other than the Rajputs of 'Avanti' in Malwa."

The Assyrians, too, were of Indian origin. Their first king was Bali, Boal or Bel, This Boal or Bali was a great king of India in ancient times. He ruled from Cambodia to Greece. Professor Maurice says: "Bali.....was the puissant sovereign of a mighty empire extending over the vast continent of India."

Mr. Pococke says, "Thus, then, at length, are distinctly seen – firstly, the identical localities in the Indian and Tartarian provinces whence Palestine was colonised; secondly, the identity of idolatry is proved between India, the old country, and Palestine the new; thirdly, the identity of the Rajput of India and of Palestine; fourthly, the positive notification of the distinct tribe which the Israelites encountered and overthrew."

XIII

Indian Origin
of
Civilisation in Turkistan and Northern Asia

The Turanians extending over the whole of Turkistan and Central Asia were originally an Indian people. Coionel Tod says: "Abdul Gazi makes Tamak, the son of Ture, the Turishka of the Purāṇas. His descendants gave their name to Tocharistan or Turkistan." Max Müller says: "Turvas and his descendants who represent Turaninas are described in the later epic poems of India as cursed and deprived of their inheritance," and hence their migration.

Colonel Tod says: "The Jaisalmer annals assert that the Yadu and the Balica branches of the Indu race ruled Korassan after the Great War, the Indo-Scythic races of Grecian authors." Besides the Balicas and the numerous branches of the Indo-Medes, many of the sons of Cooru (Kuru) dispersed over these regions: amongst whom we may place Ootooru Cooru (Uttara Kuru, i.e. Northern Kurus) of the Purāṇas, the Ottorocurae of the Greek authors. Both the Indu and the Sūrya races were eternally sending their superfluous population to those distant regions."

A Mohamedan historian says that the country of Khatha was first inhabited by a body of emigrants from India.

According to Harivaṁśa Purāṇa (Viṣṇu Parva,

Adhyāya 97), "A band of Indian settlers left India for Siberia, where they founded a kingdom, with Bajrapur as its capital. It is related that on the death of the king of that country in a battle, Pradyumna, Gāda and Sāmbha, three sons of Śri Krishna, with a large number of Brahmans and Kṣatriyas, went there, and the eldest brother succeeded to the throne of the deceased Rājā. On the death of Śri Krishna they paid a condolence visit to Dvārakā."

Colonel Tod says: "The annals of the Yadus of Jaisalmer state that long anterior to Vikrama, they held dominion from Ghazni to Samarkand; that they established themselves in those regions after the *Mahābhārata* or the Great War, and were again impelled on the rise of Islamism within the Indus. He further says, "They claim Chaghtaes as of their own Indu stock, "a claim which, "says Colonel Tod, "I now deem worthy of credit."

The Afghans are the decendants of the Aphgana, the serpent tribe of the Apivansa of ancient India. "According to Abu Haukal (quoted by Tod), the city of Herat is also called Heri. This adjoins Maru or Murve." The country called Seestan, which the Middle Eastern Question may yet bring more prominently before the public, was a settlement of the Indians. Colonel Tod says: "Seestan (the region of cold, seesthan) and both sides of the valley were occupied in the earliest periods by another branch of the Yadus." Again he says, "To the Indu race of Aśva (the descendants of Deomida and Bajaswa), spread over the countries on both sides of the Indus, do we owe the distinctive appellation of Asia."

That the Bactrians were an Indian people has already been shown. And that the Indian migrations extended to Siberia and the northern-most part of Asia is evident from the fact that the descendants of the Aryan migrators are still found there.

According to Tod, "The Samoyedes and Tchoudes of Siberia and Finland are really Soma-yadus and Joudes of India. The languages of the two former races are said to have a strong affinity and are classed as Hindu-Germanic by Klaproth, the author of 'Asia Polyglotta'." Mr. Remusat traces these tribes to Central Asia, where the Yadus long held sway. Sama, Shyam is a title of Krishna. They were Sama Yadus.

XIV
Indian Origin
of
Civilisation in Eastern Asia

According to Harbilas Sarda :

The eastward wave of Indian emigration covered the whole of Eastern Asia, comprising the Transgangetic Peninsula, China, Japan; the isles of the Indian Archipelago, Australia, and broke upon the shores of America.

The manners and institutions of the inhabitants of the Transgangetic Peninsula bear so strong an affinity to those of the Indians that one cannot resist the idea of their having been a Indians at some distant period. The fundamental principles which underlie their polity, manners, morality and religion are the same as those of the Indians. In fact, it may be taken for granted that the Trangangetic Peninsula was but a part and parcel of India so far as society, religion and polity were concerned. There was no general change in India but was also wrought there. The propagation of Buddhism was not confined to India; the people of the Transgangetic Peninsula took their share in it.

Till recently the Peninsula was swayed wholly by Indian thought but by and by a second power was felt to assert itself. China accepted the religion of the Great Buddha. Thenceforward it became a rival power with India in the eyes of the inhabitants of the Peninsula. The Aryas soon reverted to their ancient faith, or rather to a modified form of the ancient faith, but on the people of the Peninsula the grasp of the reformed faith was too firm to be easily shaken off, and hence the silver cord of friendship that tied two together was

snapped. The inhabitants of the Transgangetic
Peninsula thenceforward began to look up to the
Celestials rather than to the Indians for enlightenment
and instruction. But as their political and social
institutions had a Hindu a total overthrow of Indian
system in consequence of this cleavage was impossible.
Their civilisation therefore retained its Indian basis.

It is a well-known fact that the Pardah system was
unknown in ancient India and that it came in the train
of the Mohamedan invaders. The present position of the
Burmese women in the social and domestic life of
Burma, supports the theory that the Celestial influence
over the countries between the Brahmaputra and the
Pacific was too strong and deep to allow the people
there to follow the Hindus in their revolutionary social
changes that were unhappily forced upon them by the
wave of a less civilised but a more determined foreign
aggression.

"The Burmans, we are told by Symes, as quoted by
Harbilas Sarda, call their Code generally, Dharmasath or
Sāstra; it is one among the many commentaries on Manu.
Mr. Syme speaks in glowing terms of the Code."

Mr. Wilson as quote by Haibilas Sarda says: "The
civilisation of the Burmese and the Tibetans is derived
from India."

Harbilas Sarda says, "The name Burma itself is of
Indian derivation and proves the Indian origin of the
Burmans. The name Camboja is frequently mentioned in
Sanskrit works, and who that has read accounts of it will
deny its identity with Cambodia? In 1882 a Hindu temple
was excavated in that country by Frenchman. whose
writings prove that in ancient times, if not a part of the
Indian empire, it was most closely connected with it."

According to the same author, "China, too, was a

colony of the ancient Indians. According to the Hindu theory of emigration, China was first inhabited by the Kṣatriyas from India." Colonel Tod says: " The genealogists of China and Tartary declare themselves to the descendants of "Avar," son of the Hindu King, "Pururvā."

Sir W. Jones says, "The Chinese assert their Indian origin."

According to the traditions noted in the *Schuking*, the ancestors of the Chinese conducted by Fohi came to the plains of China 2900 years before Christ, from the high mountain land which lies to the west of that country. This shows that the settlers into China were originally inhabitants of Kashmir, Laddakh, Little Tibet, and Punjab, which were parts of ancient India.

The religion and culture of China are undoubtedly of Indian origin. Count Bjornstjerna says, "What may be said with certainty is that the religion of China came from India."

Harbilas Sarda says, "That ancient India had constant intercourse with China no one can deny. China and Chinese product are constantly mentioned in the Indian literature. For example, Rāmāyaṇa mentions Chinese silk and other manufactures. Chinese authors, too, according to Elphinstone, note Indian ambassadors to court of China. Heeren says that the name China is of Indian origin and came to us from India."

The wave of Indian migration before breaking on the shores of America submerged the islands of the Indian Archipelago. Colonel Tod says, "The isles of the Archipelago were colonised by the Sūryas (Sūrya-Vaṁśa, Kṣtriyas) whose mythological and heroic history is sculptured in their edifices and maintained in their writings."

Mr. Elphinstone says : "The histories of Java give a distinct account of a numerous body of Hindus from Kalinga who landed on their island, civilised the inhabitants and established an era still subsisting, the first year of which fell in the seventy fifth year before Christ."

The colonisation of the eastern coast of Java" by Brahmans is "a fact well established by Sir Stamford Raffles as quoted by Heeren.

Later immigrants from India were evidently Buddhists. Mr. Sewell (*Antiquarian Notes in Java*, Journal R.A.S, p.402 (1906) quoted by Harbilas sarda says, "Native tradition in Java relates that about the beginning of the seventh century (603 AD according to Fergusson) a prince of Gujrat arrived in the island with 5,000 followers and settled at Mataram. A little later 2,000 more immigrants arrived to support him. He and his followers were Buddhists, and from his time Buddhism was firmly established as the religion of Java."

"The Chinese pilgrims who visited the island in the fourth century found it entirely peopled by Indians," Respecting the inhabitants of Java, Mr. Buckle says: "Of all the Asiatic islanders this race is the most attractive to the imagination. They still adhere to the Hindu faith and worship."

Dr. Cust (as quoted by Harbilas Sarda, p. 149, footnote 7) says, "In the third group we come once more on trace of the great Aryan civilisation of India; for many centuries ago some adventurous Brahmans from the Telegu coast (or from Cambodia) conveyed to Java their religion, their sacred books and their civilisation, and Java became the seat of a great and powerful Hindu dynasty. As regards Borneo the largest island of the Archipelago, another traveller observes that "in the very inmost recesses of the mountains as well as over the face of the country, the remains of temples and pagodas are to be seen similar to those found on the continent of India bearing all the traits of Hindu mythology; and that in the country of Wahoo, at least 400 miles from the coast, there are several of very superior workmanship with all the emblematic figures so common in Hindu places of worship."

Sir Stamford Raffles (Description of Java, Vol II p. 236) while describing the small island of Bali, situated towards the east of Java says: "Here, together with the Vedic religion, is still preserved the ancient from of Hindu municipal polity."

According to Harbilas Sarda, "The Bugis of the island of *Celebes* trace back their history to the Savira Geding, whom they represent to have proceeded in immediate descent from their heavenly mediator Baitara Guru (which is distinctly a Hindu name), and to have been the first chief of any celebrity in Celebes."

As regard Sumatra, M. Coleman (Hindu Mythology. p. 361) says, "Mr. Anderson in his account of his mission to the coast of that island (Sumatra) has, however, stated that he discovered at Jambi the remains of an ancient Hindu temple of considerable dimensions, and near the spot various mutilated figures, which would appear to clearly indicate the former existence of the worship of the Vedantic philosophy."

Harbilas Sarda observes that Australia was probably deserted soon after its settlement. But that the wave of Hindu civilisation and emigration did at one time break on the shores of Australia is evident from the fact that many extraordinary things are found there. Among other things, the native races have got a kind of arrow, which clearly betrays its Indian origin. This arrow called bomerang by the native, is exactly the same as that used by Arjuna and Karana in the Mahābhārata. Its great merit is that it returns to the archer if it misses the aim."

XV
Indian Origin
of
Civilisation in Germany

That the Ancient Germans were migrators from India is proved by the following passage from Muir that approved in Manning's Ancient and Mediaevel India Vol, I, p.118 : " It has been remarked by various authors (as Kuhn and Zeitschrift, IV. 94 ff.) that in analogy with Manu or Manus as the father of mankind or of the Aryas, German mythology recognises Manus as the ancestor of Teutons." The English 'man' and the German 'mann' appear also to be akin to the word 'manu', and the Geman 'mensch' presents a close resemblance to 'manush' of Sanskrit."

The first habit of the Germans, says Tacitus, on rising was ablution, which Colonel Tod thinks must have been of Eastern origin and not of the cold climate of Germany as also "the loose flowing robe, the long and braided hair tied in a knot at the top of the head so emblematic of the Indians."

The Germans are the Sharmans of India. Sharman became Jarman and Jarman became Jerman, as Arya, Arjya and Arshya (see Max Müller's *Rgveda*). Csoma-De-Coras in the Preface to his Tibetan Dictionary, says, "The Hungarians will find a fund of information from the study of Sanskrit respecting their origin, manners, customs and language."

The Saxons are no other than the sons of the Śakas, Śakas, who lived on the North-western frontier of Āryāvartta, whence they migrated to Germany. The name

Saxon is a compound of "Saca" (Śakas) and "sanu" (descendants). They were so-called because they were descendants of the Śakas. Their name for Heaven is the same as that of the Indians. A critic says: "It is from the Himalayan Mountains of the Sacas that the 'Sac-soons' those sons of the Sacas (Saxons or Sacsons, for the words are at once Sanskrit, Saxon and English) derived their Himmel or Heaven."

Colonel Tod (Tod's Rajasthan, People's Edition, vol.1, p. 520) says, "I have often been struck with a characteristic analogy in the sculptures of the most ancient Saxon cathedrals in England, and on the continent to Kanhaiya and the Gopis. Both may be intended to represent divine harmony. Did the Asi and Jits of Scandinavia, the ancestors of the Saxons, bring them from Asia?"

XVI
Indian Origin
of
Scandinavian Civilisation

The Scandinavians are the descendants of the Indian Kṣatriyas. The term Scandinavian and the Indian "Kṣ atriya" are identical, "the former being a Sanskrit equivalent for the latter:" "Scanda Nabhi" (Scanda Navi) signifies Scanda Chiefs (Warrior Chiefs)

Colonel Tod says: "The Aśvas were chiefly of the Indu race, yet a branch of the Sūryas also bore this designation." In the Edda we are informed that the Getes or Jits who entered Scandinavia were termed Asi, and their first settlement was Asigar (Asi garh, fortress of the Asi)."

Pinkerton, as quoted by Tod, says, "Odin came into Scandinavia in the time of Darius Hystaspes, 500 years before Christ, and that his successor was Gotama. This is the period of the last Buddha, or Mahavira, whose era is 477 before Vikrama, or 533 BCE., Gotama was the successor of Mahavir."

"In the martial mythology and warlike poetry of the Scandinavians a wide field exists for assimilation.

"We can scarcely question," says Count Bjornstjerna, "the derivation of the Edda (the religious book of ancient Scandinavia) from the Vedas."

The principles on which the seven days of the week are named in India is the same on which it has been done in Scandinavia:-

(1) Sunday is called by the Indians as *Ādityavāram*, after Aditi the sun, after which also the Scandinavians call the day Sondag.

(2) Monday is called by the Indian *Somavāram*, from Soma, the moon. Among the Scandinavians it is called Mondag.

(3) Tuesday is called *Mangalavāram* in India after the Hindu hero, Maṅgala. It bears the name Tisdag amongst the Sacndinavians, after their hero, This.

(4) Wedensday is termed *Buddhavāram* by the Hindus, after Buddha; by the Scandinavians, it is denominated after Oden (Wodan, Bodham, Budha), Onsdag.

(5) Thursday is called *Bṛhaspativāram* by the Indians, after Bṛahaspati, their principal god; it bears the name Thorsdag amongst the Scandinavians, after their principal god, Thor.

(6) Friday is called by the Indians *Śukravāram*, after Śukra the goddess of beauty; it is named by the Scandinavians after Freja, the goddess of beauty, Frejdag.

(7) Saturday is called *Śanivāram* by the Indians after Śanaiścara, the god who cleanses spiritually; it is named Lordag by the Scandinavians from loger, bathing.

"We have here," says Count Bjornstjerna himself a Scandinavian gentleman, "another proof that the Myths of the Scandinavians are derived from those of the Indians."

XVII
Indian Origin
of
Hyperborean Civilisation

According to Pococke, the Hyperboreans (who formerly occupied the Northern most parts of Europe and Asia) were the Khyberpurians, or the inhabitants of Khyberpur and its district. Another Khyber settlement will be seen in Thessaly on the Eastern branch of Phoenix river. Its name is tolerably well-preserved as Khyphara and Khyphera.

Mr. Pocoke says: "While the sacred tribe of Dado, or the Dadan, fixed their oracle towards the northerly line of the Hellopers, in Thessaly, the immediate neighbours of the Hyperboreans took up their abode towards the south of the holy mountain of To-Maros, or Soo-Meroo (Sumeru). These were the Pashwaran, or the emigrants from Peshawar, who appear in the Greek guise of Passaron. We now readily see the connection between the settlements of the Dodan (Dodanian Oracle), Passaron (Peshawar people), and the offerings of the Hyperboreans, or the men of Khyberpur, who retained this appellation wherever they subsequently settled.

XVIII
Indian Origin
of
Civilisation in Great Britain

According to Harbilas Sarda, "The Druids in ancient Britain were Dardas of India who adopted the metempsychosis, the pre-existence of the soul, and its return to the realms of universal space. They had a divine triad, consisting of a Creator, Preserver, and Destroyer, as with the Dardas. The Druids constituted a Sacerdotal Order which reserved to itself alone the interpretation of the mysteries of religion."

Mr. Pococke says, "It was the Macedonian hero who invaded and vanquished the land of his forefathers unwittingly. It was a Napier who, leading on the small but mighty army of Britain, drove into headlong flight the hosts of those warlike clans from whose parent stock himself and not a few of his troops were the direct descendants."

Mr. Pococke also says, "The Scotch clans, their original localities and their chiefs in Afghanistan and Scotland, are subjects of the deepest interest. How little did the Scotch officers who perished in the Afghan campaign think that they were opposed by the same tribes from whom they themselves sprang! A work on this subject is in progress."

Mr. Pococke says, "It is in no spirit of etymological trifling that I assure the reader, that the far-famed 'hurrah' of his native country (England) is the war cry of his forefather, the Rajput of Britain, for he was long the denizen of this island. His shout was 'haro! haro! (hurrah!

hurrah!) Hark to the spirit-stirring strains of Wordsworth, so descriptive of this Oriental warrior. It is the Druid who speaks :

> "Then seize the spear, and mount the scythed wheel,
> Lash the proud steed, and whirl the flaming steel,
> Sweep through the thickest host and scorn to fly,
> Arise! arise! for this it is to die,
> Thus, neath his vaulted cave the Druid sire
> Lit the rapt soul, and fed the marital fire."

"The settlement of the people of the Draus in this island, the northern part of which was essentially that of the HI-BUDH-DEES (E-BUDH-DES,) or the land of the Hiya Buddhas at once account satisfactorily for the amazing mechanical skill displayed in the structure of Stone Henge, and harmonises with the industrious and enterprising character of the Buddhists throughout the old world; for these are the same people who drained the valley of Kashmir, and in all probability the plains of Thessaly."

The history of the Druids is thus explained: "The Druids were Drui-des. They were in fact the same as the Druopes. These venerated sages, chiefs of the tribes of the Draus, were, of the Indu Vaṁsa or lunar race. Hence the Symbol of the crescent worn by these Druids. Their last refuge in Britain from the oppression of the Romans was 'the Isle of Saints' or 'Mona' (more properly 'Mooni' Sanskrit for a holy sage). The Druids were the bards of the ancient Rajputs."

> Hark!'t was the voice of harps that poured along
> The hollow vale the floating tide of song:
> I see the glittering train, in long array,
> Gleam through the shades, and snowy splendours play;
> I see them now with measured steps and slow,
> 'Mid arching groves the white-robed sages go.
> The caken wreath with braided fillet drest---

The crescent beaming on the holy breast----
The silver hair which waves above the lyre,
And shrouds the strings, proclaim the Druid's quire.
They halt and all is hushed.

That the Indians inhabited Britain first in ancient times is clear from the fact that a chief of the twice born was once brought form Śaka-dvipa (Britain) to India by Viṣṇu's Garuḍa!

Godfrey Higgins in "Cletic Druids," has given evidence of Indian colonisation of Great Britain. According to him, Druids were the Daradas mentioned by Manu who emigrated from India and settled in Britain.

XVIX
Indian Origin
of
American Civilisation

Extensive remains of cities which must have been once in a most flourishing condition, of strong and well-built fortresses, as well as the ruins of very ancient and magnificent buildings, tanks, roads and canals that meet the eye over a very wide area of the southern continent of America, irresistibly force one to the conclusion that the country must have been inhabited at one time by a very highly civilised race

The researches of European antiquarians trace American origin to India. According to Coleman, "Baron Humboldt, the great German traveller and scientist, describes the existence of Hindu remains still found in America. Speaking of social usages of the inhabitants of Peru, Mr. Pococke says, "The Peruvians and their ancestors, the Indians, are in this point of view at once seen to be the same people."

The architecture of ancient America resembles the Indian style of Architecture. Mr. Hardy says, "The ancient edifices of Chichen in Central America bear a striking resemblance to the tops of India." Mr. Squire also says: "The Buddhist temples of Southern India, and of the islands of the Indian Archipelago, as described to us by the learned members of the Asiatic Society and the numerous writers on the religion and antiquities of the Hindus, correspond with great exactness in all their essential and in many of their minor feature with those of Central America. Dr. Zerfii remarks: "We find the remarkable temples, fortresses, viaducts, aqueducts of the Aryan group."

Harbilas Sarda says that a still more significant fact proves Indian origin of civilisation of ancient America. The mythology of ancient America furnishes sufficient grounds for the inference that it was a child of Indian mythology. The following facts will elucidate the matter :

(1) Americans worshipped Mother Earth as a mythological deity, as the Indian still do – *dharati mātā* and *pṛthivi mātā* are well-known and familiar phrases in Indian.

(2) Footprints of heroes and deities on rocks and hills were worshipped by the Americans as devoutly as they are done in India even at the present day. Mexicans are said to have worshipped the footprints of Quetzal Coatle, as the Indians worship the footprints of Buddha in Ceylon, and on Krishna in Gokula near Mathura."

(3) The Solar and Lunar eclipses were looked upon in ancient America in the same light as in India. The Indian beat drums and make noises by beating tin pots and other things. The Americans, too, raise a frightful howl and sound musical instruments. The Carecles (Americans) think that the demon "Maleoyo, the hater of light, swallows the moon and the sun in the same way as the Indian think that the demons *Rahu* and *Ketu* devour the sun and the moon.

(4) The Priests were represented in America with serpents round their heads, as Śiva, Kāli and others are represented in India.

(5) The Mexicans worshipped the figure made of the trunk of a man with the head of an elephant. The Indians, as is too well-known, still worship this deity under the name of Gaṇesh. Baron Humboldt thus remarks on the

Mexican deity: "It presents some remarkable and apparently not accidental resemblance with the Hindu Ganesh."

(6) The legend of the Deluge, as believed in by the Indians, was also prevalent in America.

(7) The Americans believed that the sun stood still at the word of one of their saints. In mediaeval India also, it is said to stand still.

(8) The tortoise myth is common to India and America. Mr. Tyler says, "The striking analogy between the tortoise myth of North America and India is by no means a matter of new observation; it was indeed noticed by Father Lafitan nearly a century and a half ago. Three great features of the Asiatic stories are found among the North American Indians in their fullest and clearest development. The earth is supported on the back of a huge floating tortoise, the tortoise is conceived as being itself the earth floating upon the face of the deep."

(9) The serpent-worship was common to both countries. In India, even to the present day, the serpent is the emblem of wisdom, power, duration, life, eternity and a symbolic representation of the sun. The fact that serpent-worship is common to the Hindu, the Egyptian, the Syrian, the Grecian, the Chinese, the Scandinavian and the American mythologies has been held to be another proof of the Indian mythology being the parent of these systems of mythology. Their philosophy was also derived from India. Their belief in the doctrine of the transmigration of souls stamp their philosophy also as being of Indian origin.

Apart from mythology, the manners, customs and habits of the ancient Americans bore a very close resemblance to those of the Hindus. Their dress, costume, and sandals prove them.

XX

Mediaeval Indian Custom
of
Devadāsī (Virgin of the Temple)
Preserved by All Ancient Countries

We shall be brief on the points for consideration suggested by the matters of this chapter, which would easily open to door to elaborate study of all ancient worships. It is scarce necessary to say such is not our object.

After having, to the best of our ability, proven the influence of India on all antique societies, by its legislation, its science, moral and philosophy; proven that the impotence, the degradation, and the fall of ancient civilisation, had no other cause than corruption of the religious idea by those especially who ought to have presented it to the people in all its divine purity; after having demonstrated the identity of origin of all the nations of the white race, by the unity of idea of all the great principle that pervaded the ancient world; we would now simply intimate that in farther examining these principles, in studying them in all their relative details, in all the results they produce, we shall find the same points of contact, the same points of logical resemblance, betraying a filiation that ascends to the remote myths and legends of the Indians.

The Devadāsī, in mediaeval ages in India, were virgins attached to the service of pagodas and temples, and whose functions were as various as they were numerous. Some tended the sacred fire that burned day and night before the symbolic statue of the Holy Trinity

(*Trimūrtī*) – Brahma,　　Viṣṇu and Śiva. Others, on the days of procession, danced before the car or ark, which carried through the villages and the country, either the statue of this Trinity or those of the three persons composing it.

There are others, whose, mission is to sing sacred hymns of rejoicing and happiness at family sacrifices and festivals. Their presence was also necessary at those funeral ceremonies which religion required each sort to accomplish at the death, and on each recurring anniversary of the death, of his father and of his mother.

Kings, on the eve of a battle, or of any other great event consulted those who received the revelations of the Divinity and piously followed their oracles, which always thus commenced.

These Indian customs doubtless accompanied emigrations, and to them should be attributed the employment of women in all the mysteries of antiquity.

According to Louis Jacolliot, "The consecrated virgins of Egypt, who danced before the statue of gods, the Phythonesses of Delphi, the priestesses of Ceres, who delivered oracles, the vestals of Rome who tended the sacred fire, were but heirs of the Devadāsī of India; absolute identity of role and of attributes, render any other conclusion impossible."

She further says :

This tradition of the woman, virgin and priestess, is so much mediaeval Indian importation.

No more than other people of antiquity, could the Hebrews escape beliefs, then general; and the Bible informs us, that Saul, on the eve of the battle of Gilboa, went to consult the Witch of Endor, who made the ghost of Samuel the Prophet appear to him.

We many argue, discuss, deny, but we dare assert, shall not disprove this influence of India on the world, which reappears at each step, in great principles, as in the details of their application.

Very certainly, these Devadāsī, these Pythonesses, these consecrated virgins, and these vestals, were, in antiquity, as in India of post *Mahābhārata* period. Here it may be noted that the prevalence of post *Mahābhārata* period Indian customs in European countries proves the fact that these customs went there with Indian immigrants who migrated European countries after the war of *Mahābhārata*

XXI

Indian Origin
of
Civilisation in Palestine

It is well known that in India there was a great dynasty famous as 'Maurya'. King Ashoka was a famous emperor from this dynasty. He had sent scholars to spread Buddhism in the western countries as well as the eastern countries. Those preachers had gone to Egypt, Syria, Palestine, Aepirus, Greece, Macidona, etc. Bauddha was a philosophical religion which was difficult to understand to uncultured and nomadic people, because it was full of the commandments like Truth, Non-violence etc. If such nomads, uncultured people inhabited the western territories upto Greece, it was futile to preach such a high grade philosophy to them. But it was not the case. Indians were there and the Vedic religion embraced the best philosophy and ethics. Therefore it is evident that the people there were capable to learn and understand the language and concepts of Bauddha preachers. In the Christ Church, Psalm 68-31, in the common prayer 'Morians' are referred to. European scholars connected Morians to Abisinia. But it is important to note that in the Bible those original Aramaic words are kept intact, because of their significance and auspicious nature. In its translations also, those words are kept intact. They are still present in Tamilnadu state of India, in the Tamil language, even though two thousand years have passed. These words are spoken and written in the present Tamil. Therefore, it is evident that Aramaic language is a corrupt form of Tamil. It is for this reason that the Morians mentioned in Aramaic language are the famous Mauryas of India. It is also natural that the Mauryas are mentioned in the Bible by the Indian people. There should not be any doubt in mind to accept this fact.

It is stated above that the words uttered by legendary Christ are preserved in the original form in the Bible as well as in its translation. For example, let us see here some words. In the Bible there are two words 'Korwan' and 'Korapanam', which are originally Tamil words and are corrupted in translations. In fact, these are two separate words. Korwan means the thing offered to the God or a victim offered to a deity. This word is corrupted in Aramaic to 'Korbani or Kurbani'. 'Korapanam' means a thing or money kept in front of a deity with prayer. However in the Bible's translation both the words are supposed to be a thing kept for a deity. In Tamil Korapanam or Korikkapanam means the money offered to a deity in worship. Korban = Kodubbanai is also a Tamil word. It is not necessary to tell that Tamil is converted to Aramaic. A word 'Boanerjes' means 'Vaneruje' in Tamil and both these similar words mean 'Son of Thunder producer'.

When crucified Christ allegedly said, 'Eloi, Eloi, Lama Sabacthani'. These words are almost Tamil, with a little change. The original form of this sentence is 'Eloi, Eloi, Lama Sabac tha ni.' = Eloi, Eloi, Sabac Lama thani. = The Pure Tamil sentence is , 'Eloi, Eloi, Sabikka Lamada Ni'. The meaning of this sentence is 'Oh God, why are you crushing me like this ? Why do you not take me away quickly to you?' In the modern Tamil the sentence as told by a Tamil person in Pune, according to Dr. P.V. Vartak is, 'Ennai, Sabic Lamada Ni '. Ennai = to me. Sabic = curse or crush. Lama = God. Da is a suffix showing triviality. Ni = you. Many more such similarities may be shown.

Once Aristotle was told by a Jew scholar that the Jews were Hindus. This is a very important statement, but to accept this saying as a true fact without evidence is not proper. We must find out the evidence to prove it. We must first see who were the residents of Palestine in those days. It is important to note that Indians are the first born human beings in the world and they spread and settled over different parts of globe from time to time. This fact can be verified on the basis of the cultural, social and linguistic evidences and archaeological findings that are available to prove that the entire Europe, Asia, Africa and America was inhabited by Indians. The history of these places is the History of Indian past. Palestine was also not an exception to this fact.

Below is given a comparison between the cultural tradition of India and Palestine, which will help prove the Indian origin of civilisation in Palestine. This will also help prove that the residents of Palestine were from India (particularly south India).

1] Houses of farmers of Palestine and Ceded districts of Andhra (India) are exactly similar, having flat, horizontal roofs.

2] The custom of rolling in of the mattress after getting up from sleep in the morning and spreading out a 'Chaṭai' for any guest to sit on are same in both places, among the Indians in Tamilnadu and the Arabs particularly in Palestine.

3] To prepare cakes of cow-dung and to wash clothing on the river banks with salty earth or soil is also common to both the ladies, Indian and Palestinian.

4] In ancient era, the grain was stored in special pits in the middle class and higher class houses called as 'Balada', by the Indian. The same type of pits for storing grains are present in Palestine. These pits called in Marathi as 'Balada'. They are named as 'Kulukkai or Kulumi' in Tamil.

5] For burning fire at home, sticks and wood is collected by ladies from forests, in India as well as in Palestine.

6] Filling water in vessels and carrying water-vessels on heads one above another in a row is a special style of the Indian ladies. Similarly their another style is to hold water vessel on the waist with the help of arm and forearm and a small vessel of water and a metal cup of water is held in

Fig-1

hand. Both these styles are seen among the West Asian ladies. Ladies in other countries do not use this style at all. This peculiar similarity is a proof to hold that Palestinian women were originally the south Indians. See fig.1.

7] Use of a grinding wheel of stone rotated by hands to powder grains is common in both the countries. See fig.2.

8] In the above mentioned book there are pictures of women folk in which the ladies are shown carrying water vessels on their heads (Fig.1) and their peculiar sitting style while grinding flour. (Fig.2) These styles are the same as the styles of the Indian ladies.

9] A picture of a plough seen above is exactly the same as the Indian plough.

10] While working in forest Indian women workers tie a cloth to some trees and make their children sleep in it. The same style is seen in Palestine. See figure 6.

Fig.3

11] Methods to bring down fruits like tamarind, mangoes etc. from trees is common to both the countries.

12] Race, lineage or species of dogs in Palestine is same as in India. South Indians might have taken their dogs along with them while immigrating.

Fig. 4

13] Houses in Palestine are strong like small forts and are not easily accessible. Similar were the houses in India previously.

14]It is important to note that in India as well as in Palestine, butter is not eaten as it is, but is converted to Ghee known as clarified butter and used.

15] It is a common practice to wash hands before eating, to use only the right hand for eating, to wash hands again after eating, in both the countries.

16] It is important to note that the Telugu women smoke tobacco and Palestinian women also smoke tobacco.

17] Before beginning to eat meals there is a custom to chant a name of the God in India as well as in Palestine.

Many more such similarities can be enumerated; but these are sufficient to prove that Indians inhabited Palestine.

Indian (Tamil) Origin of Aramaic

It must also be interesting to know that the language of Palestine was Aramaic and it was a version of Tamil language. In the word 'Aramaic', the suffix 'aic' is from European languages. If we remove that suffix, there only remains 'Aram'. 'Aram' itself is a short corruption of the word 'Arvam'. Arvam can be located in Tamil language. It means that the language Arvam is Tamil itself. 'Arvam' is the other name of Tamil. Therefore the Aramaic language of Palestine was Tamil. The New Testament was first written in Greek language and then translated into English. There were three languages running in Palestine. One was the regional language 'Aramaic', second was the royal language of Italy, because at that time Palestine was ruled by Rome. Third language was Greek which was honoured as a scholarly language of knowledge or literature.

In the Bible we find Arvam or Tamil names or titles in the same form or little perverted form. Some are as follows:

1)   Achar = Acharya
2)   Azaria = Acharyayya
      Ayya is a suffix to a name in Tamil.
3)   Obadiah = Upādhyāya   [
4)   Caleb = Kalappa
5)   Nagash = Nāga, cobra
6)   Nehamiah = Nahamayya
7)   Naamah = Nahamma.
8)   Merari = Murari
9)   Meremoth = Marimutthu
10)   Shallam = Selem = Selemia
11)   Ezara = Eshwara = Ishwara.
12)   Isaiah = Ishayya = Isha + Ayya.
13)   Sheva = Shiva.
14)   Shamgar = Shankar
15)   Sheshan = Shesha
16)   Jeshaih = Sheshayya
17)   Jeshab, son of Ishwara = Sheshappa.
18)   Maeseiah = Mahashaya.
19)   Rhoda = Radha
20)   Rachab = Rajappa.
21)   Simon = Sheeman=Shreeman
22)   Carmil = Carai Malai= Mountain on the seashore.
23)   Tabor = Deopuram (name of a city).
24)   Ramoh = Rampur
25)   Ramiah = Ramayya.
26)   Khilaphat = Kulapati.
27)   Sarasen = Shoorasen
28)   Muhajarin = Mahacharana. This is a name given
      to the people who left Mecca with Mohammad.
29)   Mufti = Mukhapati = Chief of men.
30)   Mahammad = Maha+Mati.= wise.
31)   Kouros = Krishna

XXII
Indian Origin
of
Civilisation in Arabia

It has already been stated that the Arabic language originated from Tamil Language of India through Aramaic. In the word 'Aramaic', the suffix 'aic' is from European languages. If we remove that suffix, there only remains 'Aram'. 'Aram' itself is a short corruption of the word 'Arvam'. Arvam can be located in Sanskrit as well as in Tamil language. 'Arvam' is also the other name of Tamil. The word 'Arav' got corrupted into 'Arab' and became the nomenclature of Arab countries and Arabic language.

Here it may be known that after *Mahābhārata* war lot of Indian Kṣatriyas who fought against Paṇḍvas left India for the fear of being prosecuted by victorious Pāṇḍavas and went to settle outside India in the areas that were already occupied by Indians in the remote past. It is quite natural. In Tamil as well as in Sanskrit language, 'Alla, Amma, Akka', are the names applied to the Goddess, who is the mother of this Universe. It was inevitable that these words went with the Indians to Arabia. In Arabia and around it, in the past Śaṅkara, Durgā, Viṣṇu were worshipped as principal deities. Thereforc the names of the these Goddesses were abundantly used by the people there. Out of these words 'Alla' is commonly used as a favourite by Muslims. Originally 'Alla' is a feminine word in Sanskrit, but Muslims use it as a masculine gender. Its meaning is supreme deity. Mohammed who introduced Muslim religion was born in a race named as

'Koresh' according to history. This race 'Koresh' was the people who were related to 'Kuru' dynasty or having Kurus as their kings, but they migrated from India to Arabia. Kuru dynasty is famous in the *Mahābhārata*. Kurus were from the race called as '*Chandra vaṁśa*' which means related to Moon, according to the *Mahābhārata*. Therefore those 'Koresh' had a sign of the Moon on their flag. The same sign of the Moon is used by Mohammed as a sign of religion. Thus the Koresh were related to Kauravas of the Lunar dynasty.

It is pertinent here to inform that the entire humankind in ancient times was classified into solar and lunar races. These solar and lunar dynasties were called as *Sūrya Vaṁśa* and *Chandra Vaṁśa* respectively. Sun is also known as 'Hema' and Moon as 'Soma'. So out side India also the human kind was divided on the same Vedic pattern as Hemitic and Semitic races after the pattern of *Sūrya Vaṁśa* and *Chandra Vaṁśas*. The Indian migrant from Solar race called themselves as Hemitic and from lunar race called themselves as Semitics. This division of humankind into Solar and Lunar races was based purely upon astronomical ground. In ancient times the calculation of the time of the entire world was done by Indians with Ujjain as 0^0 longitude. Today also we have a *Mahākāla* temple in Ujjain which signifies the Greenwich time of ancient world. The people inhabiting to the east of Ujjain were called as Solar races and to the west of Ujjain as Lunar races. In fact, the dividing line between solar and Lunar races was that East and West directions measured with Ujjain as the central point or 0^0 longitude. On account of the same reason Rama of Ayodhya was said to be Sūrya Vaṁśī and Pāṇḍavas or Kauravas of Indraprastha and Hastinapur (Delhi) were called as Chandra Vaṁśī. Since Eastern direction is dominated by Sun or Sūrya and Western direction is dominated by

Chandra or Moon. When there is Sun shining in the East, Moon reigns over the Western horizon.

Pandit Ruchiram, a member of Arya Samaj, who vouched to propagate Arya religion, had been to Arabia and roamed there for seven years in various parts of Arabia. He has written his travelogue (See G.D. Savarkar, p.25) titled as '*Seven Years in Arabia*' in which very important information is recorded. In short, it is as follows:

1] He started on foot from Karachi. He visited various places in Baluchisthan. He saw port Pasani, where are shops of the Sindhi and Gujarati Hindus. They are staying there for nearly two thousand years as recorded in the history there.

2] After Iran, he visited port Gwanar where also the Hindus are habitating for the last two thousand years. Most of them are Gujarati Hindus. Their traditions and customs are like those of Indians. Sindhi, Gujarati and Arabs are in trading.

3] At the southern coast of Arabia there is a port called as Mokalla or Mokala. Hindus are residing there for about two thousand and five hundred years. However, the trade is in hands of Indian Shia Muslims.

4] Residents of Yemen were the Hindus till the upsurge of Mohammed who established Muslim religion. Mohammed came with his followers in this province and threatened the king. He said, 'Accept me as a Paigambar and accept Muslim religion, otherwise there will be forceful conversion with bloodshed.' The king and the people were not able to defend themselves and had to bow before the Muslim invaders and embrace the Muslim religion.

5]   In Syria there is a small Hindu kingdom which is governed by French. The people call themselves 'Durja'. They are very brave. Their population is about twenty to twenty-five thousand. Pandit Ruchiram and others describe them as follows : They say they are Hindus. They keep a wad of hair, shaving the whole skull. They worship idols of the Hindu Gods and Goddesses. Their religious preceptors and spiritual teachers get livelihood through religious donations. If they meet some Hindu from India they feel great happiness and they honour him. They tell, 'In the past there was fought a great war and after it we came here to reside'. They observe that day of entry into that province as a holy, auspicious day and celebrate it. Their customs and traditions are just like the Hindus in India. In addition to the book of Pandit Ruchiram, other evidences also support this view, which is given below.

6]   Mr. Philip Smith says in his book named as '*Students Ancient History*', that the Arabs formerly shaved their heads clean keeping a tuft of hair intact, on the crown of head, called as 'Shikha'. One great warrior in the past was named as Muthapha.

7]   Dr. D.C. Oliari states in his book '*Arabia before Mohammed*' that in the Christian Patriotic literature the Arabs were said to be the Hindus.

8]   About a hundred years ago Major Wilford was told by the Hindus in India that Mecca was Hindu's holy place. In about the same period Jain people had told Dr. Buchanon that in the past, many Hindus lived in Arabia and their king Parashwa Bhattaraka ruled over Mecca.

Except these sources, ancient Indian historical sources

like *Mahābhārata, Gargasaṁhitā* and *Purāṇas* while narrating the history of Arab calls it Arbuda country which was founded by the Rajputs of Ketu Vaṁśa. After wards this territory was occupied by the Rajputs of Talajanghā clan. This state was known as Yavan after the name of Yavan, one of the heroic king of Taljanghā clan. Later on the word Yavan converted into Yaman. Yemen is still one of the states of United Arab Emirates. Arabic language is called a Yāvanī language in Sanskrit. (For detailed study readers can refer to '*Āryavarata kā prācīna itihāsa*' recently edited by present author).

The fact is that prior to the advent of Islam whole of Arabia was full of the followers of Vedas and Vedic Dharma. Bardic tribute to the four Vedas by an Arab poet, Labi-bin-e-Akhtab-bin-e-Turfa as early as 2300 years before prophet Mohammed is found on page 257 of Saerul-Okul an anthology of ancient Arabic verse. That verse with a short note on the poet has been writ largr on a column of the Yajñaśālā in the backyard of the Lakshminarayana Temple (alias Birla Temple) on the Reading Road in New Delhi.

The Arabic poem transcribed in the Roman script is as under :

> *aya muwarekal araj yushaiya noha minar Hind-e*
> *wa aradakallaha manyoni jail jikaratun.1*
> *wahalatjjali yatun ainana sahabi akha-atun jikra*
> *wahajayhi yonajjelur-raul minar HINDATUN. 2*
> *yakuluonullaba ya ahalal araj alameen kullahum*
> *fattabe-u jikaratl VEDA hukkum malam yonajjaylatun. 3*
> *wahowa alamus SAM wal YAJUR minallahay tanajeelan*
> *fa-enoma-ya akhiyo muttabay-an yobassheriyonajatun. 4*
> *wa-sai-nain humaRIG-ATHAR nasayhin ka-a-khuwatun*
> *we asanat ala-udan wahowa masha-e-ratun. 5*

A free English rendering of Labi's celebrated poem singing the praises of the Vedas goes like this :

1. Because Thou art the chosen of God blessed with divine knowledge enough; that knowledge which like four light-houses shone with such brilliance.

2. Through the (utterances of) Indian sages in four-fold abundance God enjoins on all humans to follow unhesitatingly.

3. The path of the Vedas with His divine precept lay down. Bursting with (divine) knowledge of SAM and YAJUR bestowed on creation.

4. Hence brothers respect and follow the Vedas guides to salvation. Two others - the RIG and ATHAR teach us fraternity.

5. Sheltering under their lustre dispels darkness till eternity.

Incidentally Labi's assertion that Arabs were initiated by a study of the Vedas in the Indian doctrine of human fraternity proves the Indian origin of civilisation in Arab countries.

Indian Origin of Arabian Gods

The commonly worshipped God in Arabia and around was Śaṅkar or Iśāna. Iśāna is one of the several names of Śiva. Therefore, wherever there was a reference to the God or Iśvara, it was to Śaṅkar. The son of God was famous as Skanda or Kartikeya. The name 'Skanda' was in use in Arabia and around and was corrupted to Skandar and then Kandar. The famous place Canterbury in England was Kandarpuri or Skandpuri. Skanda was converted to Kandar and then in Arabic converted to Eskandar. In India, too, those who are not in touch with Sanskrit pronounce 'Skanda' as *Iskanda, Snāna* as *Isnāna, Smaraṇa* as *Ismaraṇa, Skula* as *Iskula.* They add 'A' or 'E' before uttering 'Ska' or any other compound word or letter. We have developed this style under the Islamic influence. They said 'Snān' as 'Asnān' and

'Smaraṇa' as 'Asmaraṇa'. Therefore it is no wonder that the name 'Skanda' got converted to 'Askandar' or 'Iskandar' outside India. Skanda was the Chief General of the army of the Gods according to the *Purāṇas*. Skanda was therefore accepted as the God of war. In the west Asia and regions around it, the Divine General was supposed to be Iskandar in Arabia and in Persian language he was Sikandar. Thus Sikandar, Iskandar, Skandar etc. was Skanda or Kartikeya the son of Śankara, who was appointed as the general of army. Śankara is also known as Maheśa and Īśa in the Indian literature. This Maheśa or Īśa was worshipped commonly in the West Asia and the European territory nearby. This name 'Maheśa' got corrupted to Mozes. A book named as *'Ancient Fragments'* written by I.P. Cory tells the previous form of Moses as 'Moyeses'. Greek and other languages were close to Sanskrit, but in them the 'Visarga' took the form of 'S'. If this 'S' or 'Visarga' is removed from Moyeses the form becomes Mozes. Maheśa (Mahesh) = Mohesh=Mozes are very close to each other. 'H' is replaced by 'Y' while other parts remained the same. In Bengal Mahesh is uttered as 'Mohesh'. Similar change occured there and further Mohesh changed to Moyesh and Mozes. 'He' may be changed to 'Ye'. Let us see some more similarities now.

Indian Origin of Arabic Traditions

Below is given a comparison between the cultural tradition of India and Arabia, which will help prove the Indian origin of civilisation in Arabia. This will also help prove that the residents of Arabia were from India.

1]   In Arabia like that of India there is a strong belief that if we eat salt of a person we should not deceive him, we must be loyal to him. Similarly if we drink milk from a person we must remain loyal to him is a faith in both the Arabs and the Indians. It is supposed to be a great sin to be disloyal to salt and milk.

2] To tie small kids on back in a cloth is a fashion of the Indian women (See fig.4) but it is seen in Arabia too. A little grown up children are carried on shoulders while playing by the Indian males; the same fashion is seen in Arabia too. (See fig.5)

3] To throw a stone by a catapult or a sling is a style present in both India and Arabia.

Fig. 5

XXIII
Conclusion

In the foregoing pages, we have reviewed the influence of India on ancient civilisations.

We have explained this influence on one side, by emigrations implanting on the different soils they came to colonise, souvenirs of their language and of their social and religious institutions; and, on the other, by the sages and the legislators, who, to complete their studies, all went to the East, to seek out the origin of all science and of all tradition.

Everywhere we have seen at the head of each newly formed society, the influence of the Indian wisdom.

We have shown the ancient world, its vestiges of independence, ending, like India, of which it was an emanation, in an early old age, and a decrepitude, which had their origin in the superstition of the masses, from perversion of the religious idea.

All sublime truth on the unity of God, the Trinity, and the immortality of the soul, were withheld from them by the priests, who would have blushed to believe all the superstition which they themselves had endangered in the multitude to secure domination for their caste and their adepts.

Zoroaster doubtless intended to popularise these sublime nations, but he was cast off by his followers, and his reform only ended in a new consecration of sacerdotal power.

Buddha, too, who had preceded him, although expelled from India for his independence of thought, afterwards became, similarly, in Tibet, in China and in

Japan, a symbol of subjugation and intolerance.

These reformers were in advance of their age, and their men were not yet born. Lastly, I would like to conclude the conclusion with the following remarks of Louis Jacolliot:

> **If we have succeeded in proving that entire antiquity was, by language, usage, customs, and political traditions, but an emanation from India, who, then, will dare to cast the stone at us if we are forced, logically and fatally, to maintain, and to prove, that in India must be sought the source of primitive revelation, and of all religious traditions?**

> What! this people who so deeply stamped their traces on Persia, Egypt, Greece, and Rome, who gave these countries their language, there political organisation, their laws, would not equally have imported the religious idea?

> What! the Greek, the Latin, the Hebrew, may be born of the Sanskrit, and the ablation stop there? That is inadmissible.

> As priestly class implanted on these different soils all the superstitions, with the aid of which it had deluded and bowed the masses to its yoke, so did Manu and Manes bring with them the pure traditions of the Vedas. Which inspired the two philosophers to whom we owe the foundation of Hebrew and Christian societies.

> We shall see whence Moses exhumed his Pentateuch, that is, the first five books of the Bible, of which he is considered the author, viz., Genesis, Exodus, Leviticus, Numbers and Deuteronomy.

> When we shall have thus cleared the way, in proving that Hebrew civilisation was, like all others of ancient times, but a reflection of India, a souvenir of that common parent, we may be permitted, without fear, to

examine the role played by the Christian philosopher, who, in retaining Hebrew tradition, purified it by aid of the morale of Krishna, the great Indian reformer, which he had no doubt been able to study for himself in the sacred books of Egypt and of India.

What more natural, more simple, and more logical, than our conclusion, from the moment we energetically deny all revelation, as opposed to good sense, to reason, and to the dignity of God; from the moment we relegate all incarnations, to the domain of fable and of romance?

Ought we not to inquire if some common bond does not unite all peoples; if, in fact, in the history of past civilisations, all conquests of thought have not been connected with each other?

Have not the nineteen centuries of our modern era supported each its successor in their advance? Has not each forward step leaned for support on something already affected?

The inquirer, who, three thousand years hence, when other people have been born and other civilisations have succeeded ours, shall proclaim this truism of today, will but accomplish for our epoch, a reconstruction such as this work desires to effect for ancient times.

References

1. Buckle : *Beauties, Sublimities and Harmonies of Nature*
2. Coleman : *Hindu Mythology*
3. Count Bjornstjerna : *Theogony of Hindus*
4. (Dr.) Cust : *Linguistic and Oriental Essays*, quoted by Harbilas Sarda, p. 149. Footnote 7.
5. Cumont, Franz : *The Oriental Religions in Roman Paganism*, p. 53-57.
6. Cuvier : *Discourse* quoted by Harbilas Sarda
7. Elphinstone : *History of India*, quoted by Harbilas Sarda.

8. Eusebius : Lemp, Barker's Edition quoted by Harbilas Sarda

9. Fanny Parks : *Wonderings of a Pilgrim in Search of Picturesque*, Oxford University Press, London, 1975, p.427-432.

10. Harbilas Sarda : *Hindu Superiority*, Delhi,1906.

11. Hardy : *Eastern Monachism*

12. Hauge : Hauge's Essays on Parses.

13. (Prof.) Heeren : *Asiatic Nations*

14. (Prof.) Heeren : *Historical Researches*

15. Louis Jacolliat : *La Bible Dans L' Inde*, Paris, 1876.

16. Max Müller : *Science of Language*

17. Oak, P.N. : *World Vedic Heritage*, 3rd Ed. Delhi, 2003.

18. Pococke, E : *Indian Origin of Greece and Ancient World*, edited by Dr. Ravi Prakash Arya, IFFVS, Delhi 2004.

19. Squire : *Serpent symbol*

20. *Theosophist*, March 1881, Quoted by Harbilas Sarda

21. (Col.) Tod : *Annals of Rajasthan*

22. William Jones : *Asiatic Researches*

23. Zerfit : *A mannual of Historical development of Art.*

24. *History of China*, quoted by Harbilas Sarda

25. *Neibuhr's Rome*, Vol.1, quoted by Pococke.

-END-

www.ingramcontent.com/pod-product-compliance
Lightning Source LLC
Chambersburg PA
CBHW020038040426
42331CB00030B/33